Fodor's POCKET

Fourth edition

fodor's travel publications
new york • toronto • london • sydney • auckland

www.fodors.com

contents

maps

on the road with fodor's

A TRIP TAKES YOU OUT OF YOURSELF. Concerns of life at home completely disappear, driven away by more immediate thoughts—about, say, what marvels will beguile the next day, or where you'll have dinner. That's where Fodor's comes in. We make sure that you know all your options, so that you don't miss something that's around the next bend just because you didn't know it was there. Mindful that the best memories of your trip might have nothing to do with what you came to Aruba to see, we guide you to sights large and small all over the island. You might set out to relax in the sun on Eagle Beach, but back at home you find yourself unable to forget the breathtaking rock formations or the caves once inhabited by ancient peoples in Arikok National Park. With Fodor's at your side, serendipitous discoveries are never far away.

About Our Writer

Vernon O'Reilly-Ramesar is a radio and television broadcaster who divides his time between Toronto and the southern Caribbean. Currently based in Trinidad and Tobago, Vernon tours the region extensively for both work and pleasure. In his spare time, he enjoys exploring the miracles of Trinidad's rain forests and absorbing the complex local cultures. Vernon has contributed to Fodor's guides, including Fodor's Caribbean, for eight years.

You can rest assured that you're in good hands—and that no property mentioned in the book has paid to be included. Each has been selected strictly on its merits, as the best of its type in its price range.

be a fodor's correspondent

Your opinion matters. It matters to us. It matters to your fellow Fodor's travelers, too. And we'd like to hear it. In fact, we *need* to hear it.

When you share your experiences and opinions, you become an active member of the Fodor's community. That means we'll not only use your feedback to make our books better, but we'll publish your name and comments whenever possible.

Here's how you can help improve Fodor's for all of us.

Tell us when we're right. We rely on local writers to give you an insider's perspective. But our writers and staff editors—who are the best in the business—depend on you. Your positive feedback is a vote to renew our recommendations for the next edition.

Tell us when we're wrong. We're proud that we update most of our guides every year. But we're not perfect. Things change. Hotels cut services. Museums change hours. Charming cafés lose charm. If our writer didn't quite capture the essence of a place, tell us how you'd do it differently. If any of our descriptions are inaccurate or inadequate, we'll incorporate your changes in the next edition and will correct factual errors at fodors.com *immediately*.

Tell us what to include. You probably have had fantastic travel experiences that aren't yet in Fodor's. Why not share them with a community of like-minded travelers? Maybe you chanced upon a beach or bistro or B&B that you don't want to keep to yourself. Tell us why we should include it. And share your discoveries and experiences with everyone directly at fodors.com. Your input may lead us to add a new listing or highlight a place we cover with a "Highly Recommended" star or with our highest rating, "Fodor's Choice."

Give us your opinion instantly at our feedback center at www.fodors.com/feedback. You may also e-mail editors@fodors.com with the subject line "Aruba Editor." Or send your nominations, comments, and complaints by mail to Aruba Editor, Fodor's, 1745 Broadway, New York, NY 10019.

You and travelers like you are the heart of the Fodor's community. Make our community richer by sharing your experiences. Be a Fodor's correspondent.

Happy traveling!

Tim Jarrell,
Publisher

the caribbean

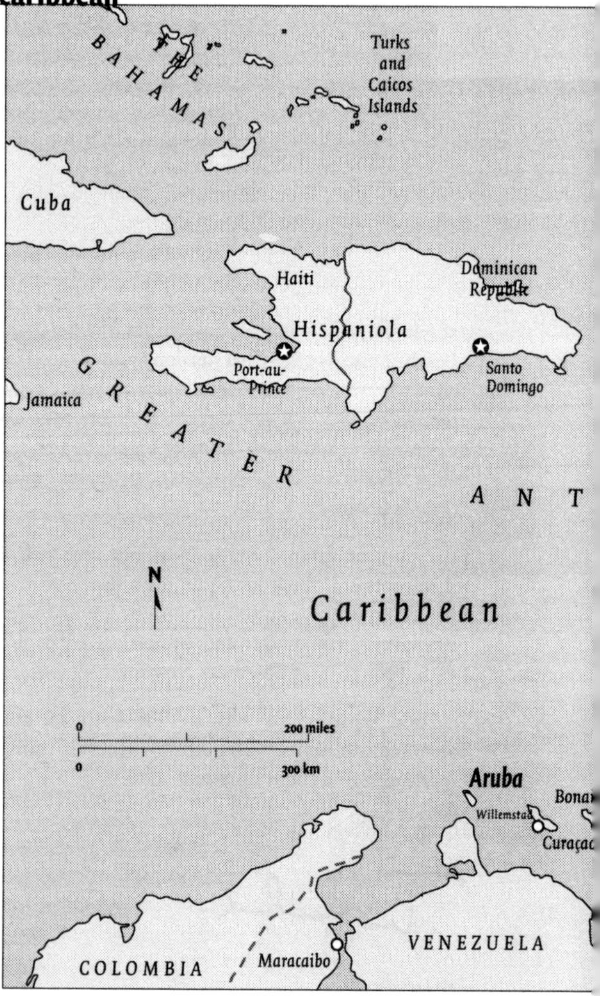

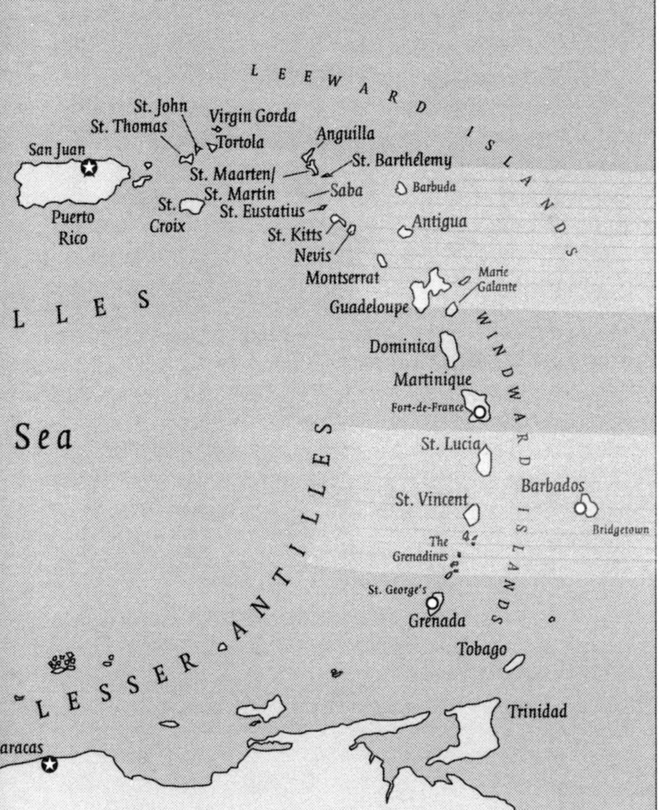
ATLANTIC OCEAN
LEEWARD ISLANDS
St. John
St. Thomas
Virgin Gorda
Tortola
Anguilla
San Juan
St. Barthélemy
St. Maarten/
St. Martin
Saba
Barbuda
St. Croix
St. Eustatius
Puerto Rico
Antigua
St. Kitts
Nevis
Montserrat
Marie Galante
Guadeloupe
LLES
WINDWARD ISLANDS
Dominica
Martinique
Fort-de-France
Sea
St. Lucia
Barbados
St. Vincent
Bridgetown
The Grenadines
St. George's
Grenada
Tobago
LESSER ANTILLES
Trinidad
Caracas

aruba

Hundreds of eager tourists disembark from a giant cruise ship in Oranjestad, streaming into the shopping area looking for bargains and a quick two-hour tour. A man stands in their way, handing out brochures for a local store—grabbing hands take them as fast as he can deliver them. As the crowds move on and the man has a chance to breathe, he turns to one of the vendors at the stall next to him. "I can't imagine being in Aruba for only a few hours" he says. "There are so many things to see, and they will miss most of them." The two Arubans shake their heads in disbelief, wondering why anyone would settle for just a taste of their beautiful island.

In This Chapter

introducing aruba

ARUBANS ENJOY LIFE—you'll see this in their gusto for food and drink, their vibrant nightlife, and mostly in their generosity of spirit. This joie de vivre is infectious; try not to have a good time mingling with locals in a bar, soaking up the sun on the beach, or dining in a fine restaurant. Aruba isn't the place to go if you're looking for a vacation off the beaten path. But for a good time, you can't go wrong in a place where the national slogan is "One Happy Island."

Aruba is the smallest member of the "ABC" islands (Bonaire and Curaçao complete the alphabetical trio). The origin of the name "Aruba" is something of a mystery, but it is thought to be Amerindian, possibly derived from the Carib word *oraoubao* (which means "shell island") or *Oruba* (which means "well located.") Some suspect that "Aruba" may have come from the Spanish phrase *oro huba* (meaning "there was gold"), but this may be a bit of a stretch. Whatever the source, the name has been in use since 1526, and a more appropriate contemporary meaning would be "the perfect vacation destination."

Once a member of the Netherlands Antilles, Aruba became an independent entity within the Netherlands in 1986. Throughout its history, the island's economy has relied on trading horses, mining gold (discovered here in 1824), cultivating aloe plants, and refining Venezuelan oil. These days, however, tourism is the primary industry, and the island's population of 100,000 treats visitors as valued guests. The national anthem proclaims, "The greatness of our people is their great cordiality," and this is no exaggeration. Waiters serve you with smiles, English is spoken everywhere, and hotel hospitality directors appear delighted to fulfill your needs.

The island's single-minded dedication to attracting tourism has resulted in a massive infrastructure. Hotels of every size line the best beaches, and entertainment is never hard to find. Glitzy casinos, high-end shops, and top-notch restaurants keep the tourist dollars flowing, but sometimes give Aruba a slightly tacky Vegas-like feel. For many, though, this only adds to the attraction. Visitors don't come to this virtual paradise to get away from it all, they're here to spend days on the beach and nights on the town. Visit, and you'll also find a warm climate, constant breezes, pristine waters fringed by idyllic beaches, and a (mostly) hurricane-free location. And of course, everywhere you look you'll see a generous and genuine Aruban smile.

THE MAKING OF ARUBA

THE PEOPLE

Archaeological and genetic research indicates that the first inhabitants of Aruba, the Caquetio people, migrated to the island as early as 2500 BC. These hunter-gatherers, who most likely arrived from the nearby Venezuelan coast, had no knowledge of agriculture or pottery-making. They seem to have settled in Aruba until about AD 1000, when another group of Caquetio people (often misspelled as Caiquetio) arrived from northwest Venezuela. This group brought with them pottery-making skills (this time is usually referred to as the Ceramic Period) and some agricultural knowledge. They spoke an Arawakan language (also called Caquetio), and DNA evidence suggests that they were closely related to Aruba's original tribal occupants. Signs of these early people can be found all over Aruba, including at the Tanki Flip archaeological site, and pottery and burial evidence suggests that they had a rich and

Islandscapes

Aruba's topography is unusual for a Caribbean island. The southern and western coasts consist of miles of palm-lined, white-sand beaches. The calm, blue-green waters are so clear that in some areas visibility extends to a depth of 100 feet. The northeast coast is wild and rugged; here the waves pound against the coral cliffs, creating remarkable rock formations. The desertlike interior is home to various types of cacti and still more extraordinary rock formations. Divi-divi trees flourish everywhere.

Poking out of the Caribbean Sea, Aruba is at latitude 12°30′ north and longitude 70° west. The island lies about 32 km (20 mi) from Venezuela's northern coast, near the Península Paraguaná. Aruba is only 32 km (20 mi) long and 10 km (6 mi) across at its widest point, with a total area of 180 square km (70 square mi).

In the east, Arikok National Park makes up 18% of the island's total area. Here you can visit 617-foot Mt. Yamanota, Aruba's highest peak. The island's capital, Oranjestad, is on the southwest coast, and Dutch and Spanish influences are evident in the colorful houses along Wilhelminastraat. Two main thoroughfares—J. E. Irausquin and L. G. Smith boulevards—link the capital to the hotels along Eagle and Palm beaches.

To the southeast lies San Nicolas, the island's second-largest metropolis and the site of an oil refinery. At Aruba's northwestern tip are large rolling sand dunes. Nestled at the island's heart, Santa Cruz is the cradle of religious culture, symbolized by a large cross marking the spot where Spanish missionaries introduced Christianity.

well-developed culture. This ended abruptly and sadly with the arrival of the Europeans.

The date when the first Europeans set foot on Aruba is unclear. Around 1499, Spanish explorer Alonso de Ojeda (a lieutenant of Christopher Columbus) explored nearby Bonaire and Curaçao, but did not mention a third island. A map created in 1502 omits Aruba, but clearly illustrates its neighbors. Aruba was first mentioned in 1505. According to oral history, an Arawak chieftain guided the first Spanish explorers inland, where they erected a cross to mark the occasion. (In 1968 this event was commemorated by the placement of a large wooden cross atop a rocky hill in Santa Cruz.) The Spanish settlers made some efforts to bring Christianity to the local population and even brought in a Christian cacique (native chief) from the mainland to assist them in their efforts.

Due to their lack of gold or other useful resources, the Spanish referred to Aruba, Bonaire, and Curaçao as "Islas Inutiles" or "useless islands." In 1513, the Spanish exported most of Aruba's native population to nearby Hispaniola (today's Dominican Republic and Haiti) to work in silver mines there. Some of the native people were brought back to the island in 1527, and others escaped to the mainland.

In 1636, during the Eighty Years' War between Holland and Spain, the Dutch took control of Aruba, Bonaire, and Curaçao, ruling them under the charter of the Dutch West India Company. Over the next 100 years, commerce grew on the island, which served as a satellite to the administrative center on larger Curaçao.

Owing to the arid climate and poor soil, Aruba was spared from plantation economics and the slave trade; instead, the Dutch used the remaining Caquetio people to herd cattle. The Dutch held power until 1805, when the English laid claim to Aruba briefly during the Napoleonic Wars. The Dutch Republic on the

European continent fell to the French in 1795, and France annexed the Netherlands in 1810. But after Napoléon's defeat in 1815, political lines throughout Europe were redrawn. The Kingdom of the Netherlands was born, and in 1816 possession of Aruba was returned permanently to the Dutch.

In 1750, Domingo Antonio Silvestre—a Venezuelan who had been converted to Catholicism by Spanish missionaries—built a small chapel at Alto Vista on the island's north shore to accommodate the Catholic community, which until this time had had no formal place of worship. The winding approach road is lined with 12 white crosses indicating the stations of the cross, which pilgrims can follow to the tranquil chapel. The church of Santa Ana, built in the district of Noord in 1776, is renowned for its handsomely carved oak altar, which was awarded a prize for neo-Gothic design at the Rome exhibition of 1870. Interestingly, the original 200-year-old Spanish cross from the Alto Vista chapel now resides here as well.

The first Protestant church was built in 1848 in the center of Oranjestad. Today the original building houses a museum that is maintained by the congregation; an adjoining larger church is used for weekly services. Another landmark house of worship, the Inmaculada Concepción church in Santa Cruz, is noted for the colorful biblical mural decorating its nave. The Beth Israel synagogue was built in 1962 to meet the needs of the growing Jewish community. (A congregation began forming as early as the 1920s, when an international workforce was drawn to Aruba to staff the oil refinery.)

With a history full of cultures clashing and melding, it's no surprise that most islanders are fluent in several languages. School lessons are taught in Dutch, the official language. Arubans begin studying English, recognized as the international tongue, beginning in the fourth grade. Spanish, essential because of Aruba's proximity to South America, is taught in school as early as fifth grade, and French is offered as an option in high school. In normal conversation, however, the locals speak Papiamento—a mix of Spanish, Dutch, Portuguese, English, and French, as well as Indian and African languages. Since 1998, Papiamento has also been taught in grade school.

THE ECONOMY

Due to its dry climate and poor soil, Aruba was basically unused by the colonists until the Dutch introduced horses and cattle. They enlisted the locals to be herders, and Aruba was a convenient livestock and meat depot for many years. As more colonists arrived from Curaçao and Brazil in the 1700s, the economy began a lazy evolution. Then, in the 19th century, Aruba's cycle of boom and bust began with the discovery of gold in Rooi Fluit in 1824. The ensuing rush helped breathe new life into the sleepy island.

The gold industry exploded and the population swelled as immigrants flowed in from neighboring islands and the mainland. Aruba soon became an important supplier of gold, and by 1916—when supplies were depleted—close to 3 million pounds of gold had been extracted. The remnants of the gold industry can still be seen at the gold-smelter ruins in Bushiri. During the time of the gold rush, the island also became a major supplier of aloe vera, divi-divi pods (used for tanning leather), and calcium phosphate. These industries, however, were not able to support the economy after the gold industry closed, and the island fell into another slump.

Aruba ended this economic downturn by opening an oil refinery. Though the island has no oil resources of its own, it is well positioned to be a processing and shipment point for oil from Venezuela. In 1926 workers began blasting away the reef on the southern coast near San Nicholas, and the harbor was dredged to allow large ships to enter. Then, in 1928, the Royal Dutch Shell Company opened the Eagle Oil Refinery. Oil was shipped into Aruba from Lake Maracaibo in Venezuela by the Lago

Transportation Company of Canada (which eventually opened their own refinery on the island). By 1929 the new refinery was producing over 200,000 barrels a day. Huge numbers of migrant workers arrived to satisfy the demands for labor, which helped fuel a population boom and added to an increasingly cosmopolitan society. At its height, the oil industry employed over 8,000 workers–about 16% of the island's population.

The importance of Aruba's oil refining was made obvious during WWII. Aruba, Curaçao, and the nearby British island of Trinidad were key Ally supply depots in the Caribbean, and German U-boats were sent to close them down. In 1942, the harbor and the Lago refinery at San Nicholas were bombed. Two tankers were hit by torpedoes, but an accident aboard the German U-156 disabled its deck guns, and the refinery was spared. There is no doubt that Hitler, at the time, viewed the destruction of Aruba's oil production as a key strategy for winning the war. The oil industry continued to grow despite the threats of attack, reaching a peak production of 550,000 barrels a day in 1965.

Because of an unstable oil market, the refinery was closed in 1985. The Coastal Corporation of Texas reopened it in 1991 (and it now produces 150,000 barrels a day), but the tourist trade has replaced oil as Aruba's primary source of income. Education, health care, and other public services are financed by tourism, which has also helped to keep the unemployment rate at less than 1%. Because of this, it's no surprise that guests are warmly received. This warmth has, in turn, contributed to a general upward trend in the number of visitors—from 206,750 in 1985 to more than 800,000 in 2004.

THE GOVERNMENT

Until late 1985 Aruba was a member of the Netherlands Antilles, along with Bonaire, Curaçao, St. Maarten, St. Eustatius, and Saba. On January 1, 1986, Aruba was granted a new status as an independent entity within the Kingdom of the Netherlands,

"Go On with the Struggle"

Arubans are proud of their autonomous standing within the Kingdom of the Netherlands, and Gilberto François "Betico" Croes is heralded as the hero behind the island's status aparte (separate status). His birthday, January 25, is an official Aruban holiday.

During the Dutch colonial expansion of the 17th century, Aruba and five other islands—Bonaire, Curaçao, St. Maarten, St. Eustatius, and Saba—became territories known as the Netherlands Antilles. After World War II, these islands began to pressure Holland for autonomy, and in 1954 they became a collective self-governing entity under the umbrella of the Kingdom of the Netherlands.

At that time, several political parties were in power on the island. Soon, however, Juancho Irausquin (who has a major thoroughfare named in his honor) formed a new party that maintained control for nearly two decades. Irausquin was considered the founder of Aruba's new economic order and the forebearer of modern Aruban politics. After his death, his party's power diminished.

In 1971 Croes, then a young, ambitious school administrator, became the leader of another political party. Bolstered by a thriving economy generated by Aruba's oil refinery, Croes spearheaded the island's cause to secede from the Netherlands Antilles and to gain status as an equal partner within the Dutch kingdom. Sadly, he didn't live to celebrate the realization of his dream. On December 31, 1985, the day before Aruba's new status became official, Croes was in a car accident that put him in a coma for 11 months. He died on November 26, 1986. Etched in the minds of Arubans are his prophetic words: "Si mi cai na cominda, gara e bandera y sigui cu e lucha" *("If I die along the way, seize the flag and go on with the struggle").*

which now consists of the Netherlands, the Netherlands Antilles, and Aruba.

The island has a royally appointed governor, who acts as the Dutch sovereign's representative for a six-year term. Executive power is held by the seven-member council of ministers, appointed by the legislative council for four-year terms and presided over by the prime minister, who is elected every four years. The legislature consists of a parliament whose 21 members are elected by popular vote to serve four-year terms. Legal jurisdiction lies with the Common Court of Justice of Aruba and the Netherlands Antilles as well as the Supreme Court of Justice at The Hague in the Netherlands. Defense and foreign affairs still fall under the realm of the kingdom, whereas internal matters involving such things as customs, immigration, aviation, and communications are handled autonomously.

THE LANGUAGE

Papiamento is hybrid language born out of the colorful past of Aruba, Bonaire, and Curaçao. The language's use is generally thought to have started in the 17th century when Sephardic Jews migrated with their African slaves from Brazil to Curaçao. The slaves spoke a pidgin Portuguese, which may have been blended with pure Portuguese, some Dutch (the colonial power in charge of the island), and Arawakan. Proximity to the mainland meant that Spanish and English words were also incorporated.

Linguists believe the name Papiamento (a variation of Papiamentu) probably derives from the Portuguese verb *papiar*, meaning "to chatter." In Papiamento, as in some other Creole languages, the verb *papia* means "to speak." Add the suffix *mentu*, which means "the way of doing something," and you form a noun. Thus, Papiamento is roughly translated as "the way of speaking." (Sometimes the suffix *-mentu* is spelled in the Spanish and Portuguese way [*-mento*], creating the variant spelling.)

Papiamento Primer

Arubans enjoy it when visitors use their language, so don't be shy. You can buy a Papiamento dictionary to build your vocabulary, but here are a few pleasantries—including some terms of friendship and love—to get you started:

BON DIA.	*Good morning.*
BON TARDI.	*Good afternoon.*
BON NOCHI.	*Good evening/night.*
BON BINI.	*Welcome.*
AJO.	*Bye.*
TE AWORO.	*See you later.*
PASA UN BON DIA.	*Have a good day.*
DANKI.	*Thank you.*
NA BO ORDO.	*You're welcome.*
CON TA BAI?	*How are you?*
MI TA BON.	*I am fine.*
BAN GOZA!	*Let's enjoy!*
PABIEN!	*Congratulations!*
QUANTO COSTA ESAKI?	*How much is this?*
HOPI BON	*Very good*
AMI	*Me*
ABO	*You*
NOS DOS	*The two of us*
MI DUSHI	*My sweetheart*
KU TUR MI AMOR	*With all my love*
UN BRAZA	*A hug*
UN SUNCHI	*A kiss*
RANKA LENGA	*To French kiss*
MI STIMA ARUBA.	*I love Aruba.*

Papiamento began as an oral tradition, handed down through the generations and spoken by all social classes. On Aruba, you'll hear a lilting tone to the language, whereas on Curaçao, the delivery is more rapid-fire. On Bonaire, the sound is somewhere in between. There's no uniform spelling or grammar from island to island or even from one neighborhood to another.

In 1995 Aruba's citizens began a grassroots effort to raise awareness of Papiamento and to have it taught in the schools. It was made part of the curriculum in 1998; that year was also declared the Year of Papiamento in Aruba. With its official recognition, Papiamento continues to be refined and standardized. A noteworthy measure of the increased government respect for the language is that anyone applying for citizenship must be fluent in both Papiamento and Dutch.

PORTRAITS

TOURISM FACES NEW CHALLENGES

Juggling the day-to-day operations of the Aruba Tourism Authority is no easy task, but it's one that Myrna Jansen has mastered. As managing director of the ATA, she works closely with the island's minister of tourism in her efforts to attract more visitors from the United States, Canada, South America, and Europe.

The most challenging part of her job, Jansen says, is working in a world that changed so dramatically on September 11, 2001. After years of steady gains, tourism dipped. This could have been devastating for an island that relies so much on visitors' dollars. But her office shifted into high gear, getting out the message that Aruba is a safe and secure destination.

Things are looking up. The number of visitors from the United States in 2003 increased by about 6%; at the same time, the number of visitors from Europe rose by double digits. "We're heading in the right direction," says Jansen, "and it's been very rewarding."

FODOR'S: What makes Aruba a great place to vacation?

JANSEN: It's a great place to live, so it's a great place to visit. The people are always happy and we have a good quality of life, which is reflected on our tourists. We have beautiful and consistent weather; it's always 82 degrees and sunny, which has become more and more important to visitors.

FODOR'S: What do you treasure most about the island?

JANSEN: The people are something we treasure very much. Most of our visitors—about 40%—return, and many continue to visit for 30 years. They all say it's the people that make the place. I'm an Aruban and I know our hospitality shows through our interaction with visitors and through the quality of service we offer them. In addition, most Arubans are highly educated, and that brings with it a certain comfort level for visitors.

FODOR'S: Do you have a story of a special encounter with a tourist that has touched your life?

JANSEN: I met one gentleman who has been coming here for over 35 years. He always comes with a group and always stays at the same hotel, where he throws a party every year. When he speaks about why he keeps bringing people back, they are special moments that he shares with me. Also, many visitors tell us about things they feel shouldn't change because that's how they were 30 years ago. It's nice that they feel so strongly about these parts of our culture.

FODOR'S: Do you find that long-term tourists want to give back to the island?

JANSEN: There are visitors who come here and hold fund-raising events for charities like Friends of the Handicapped, which is a foundation started by tourists who wanted to give back to the island. They come every year and raise money for handicapped Arubans. Other visitors have written songs about Aruba and presented us with lyrics and music.

FODOR'S: Where are your favorite places to go on Aruba? What do you on a typical day off?

JANSEN: As a mother of three kids, I spend most of my free time with them. We usually go shopping or go to the beach, which is the most important activity for relaxation with my family. I love the part of Eagle Beach where the beach area is very wide and there are no hotels. One of my favorite sites is the north coast because it's rough and exciting. I don't get there that often, but I enjoy it when I'm there.

FODOR'S: How has Aruba changed over the past two years?

JANSEN: The only way the island has changed is that we have more activities and new places to sightsee, like the new Carnival Museum, the newly renovated Numismatic Museum, and new art galleries, most of which hold exhibitions every month and other regular events for the public.

FODOR'S: Where do you travel to on vacation and why?

JANSEN: In the past, I've been to Disney World with the kids and to Holland. I find Europe very exciting, and Holland is a gateway to Europe. My kids will go there to study, so it is important for them to feel comfortable there. Sometimes I visit other islands like Curaçao, which is only 20 minutes away, and sometimes I'll take a cruise.

FODOR'S: Describe an Aruban tradition that you cherish.

JANSEN: I cherish Dande. It's a New Year's tradition in which groups of people go from house to house singing songs that are personalized about the people living in each house. When I was

Distance Conversion Chart

KILOMETERS/MILES

To change kilometers (km) to miles (mi), multiply km by .621.

To change mi to km, multiply mi by 1.61.

KM TO MI	MI TO KM
1=.62	1=1.6
2=1.2	2=3.2
3=1.9	3=4.8
4=2.5	4=6.4
5=3.1	5=8.1
6=3.7	6=9.7
7=4.3	7=11.3
8=5.0	8=12.9

METERS/FEET

To change meters (m) to feet (ft), multiply m by 3.28.

To change ft to m, multiply ft by .305.

M TO FT	FT TO M
1=3.3	1=.30
2=6.6	2=.61
3=9.8	3=.92
4=13.1	4=1.2
5=16.4	5=1.5
6=19.7	6=1.8
7=23.0	7=2.1
8=26.2	8=2.4

very young, it was a big thing at our house and a very emotional moment for my family.

FODOR'S: Is there any message you would like to convey to vacationers about Aruba?

JANSEN: I think that Aruba can be a very active island, but a lot of visitors have the perception that there's not a lot to do here. If you're going to relax, you can always sit on the beach with a piña colada, but there are plenty of other options if you want to be active. The choice is there; it's up to you to decide what to do.

It's breakfast time at the Divi, and I drowsily glance up from my coffee. The aqua-tinted ocean sparkles as far as the eye can see, and the beach's white sand is already incandescent in the early morning sun. Pelicans sit on the mooring posts a few feet offshore, looking out for their morning meal. At this hour there are no powerboats, no laughing families—only blissful silence. I cannot imagine a more idyllic start to another perfect day in paradise.

In This Chapter

perfect days & nights

ARE YOU PERPLEXED ABOUT WHICH OF ARUBA'S MANY BEACHES is best or about how to spend your time during one of the island's rare rainy days? Below are some suggestions to guide you. There are also a few ideas on how to spend a night (or two) celebrating all the perfect days you've been having.

A PERFECT DAY AT THE BEACH

Most visitors come to Aruba to enjoy its picture-perfect beaches. Virtually every hotel on the island is either on or near an expanse of powdery white sand. Although it is possible to wander off the beaten path and find a secluded spot, the main beaches are huge, and it is almost always possible to stake out a choice location. Sunscreen is essential—keep in mind that the constant trade winds can cause you to forget the sun's intensity.

Before setting out, rent snorkel gear at your hotel so that you can fully appreciate the calm water and all its inhabitants. And why not pack a picnic? Although most hotels will prepare a basket for you, an expedition to one of the local supermarkets is more economical and offers greater variety. Ling & Sons (Italiëstraat 26, Eagle Beach) is a massive grocery store with a bakery, deli, and a staggering selection of cheeses.

For breakfast, stop at Mangos Restaurant at Amsterdam Manor for the hearty buffet—the Dutch coffee is sure to wake you up in a hurry. Eagle Beach is right across the road, and you can grab a space under one of the many palapa umbrellas if you arrive early enough. The water here is fine for swimming, and despite the busy location, you can take in some interesting sights while snorkeling. Your best bet is to spend the early part of the day in the water, while your energy level is still high.

Afternoon is the perfect time to relax, escape the heat, and snooze on a deck chair. Be sure take in liquids regularly to avoid dehydration—rum punch may sound good, but water is probably best. As the sun goes down, hop back across the road to the Pata Pata Bar at the La Cabana Resort for happy hour. The live music is always fun, and there are good drink specials. The outdoor setting is completely casual, so there's no need to change clothes.

A PERFECT RAINY DAY

Aruba has a reputation for guaranteed sunshine because of its location outside the hurricane belt. But weather patterns can be unpredictable. Here's what to do if you get caught in a storm.

Have breakfast at DeliFrance in the Certified Mega Mall on L. G. Smith Boulevard. The freshly baked bagels and the hot Dutch pancakes covered in powdered sugar will surely warm you up. By 10 AM or so, head to downtown Oranjestad to see the Archaeological Museum of Aruba, where you'll get a taste of local history from the extensive collection of Arawak artifacts, farm and domestic utensils, and skeletons. Nearby, the Numismatic Museum houses a fascinating collection of rare coins from around the world. Because you'll be in the heart of town, this is a great time to catch the mesmerizing *Experience Aruba Panorama*, a 22-minute film complete with 3-D effects and surround sound, at the Renaissance Aruba Beach Resort's Crystal Theater. Shows start every hour.

Why wait until dinner to have an elegant meal when you can have one for lunch? Make a reservation at Le Dôme, an upscale

Belgian establishment that is one of the best restaurants on the island. There are four dining rooms to choose from, but head straight to Le Gallerie to enjoy a rainy view of Eagle Beach. Whatever you choose to eat is guaranteed to be great, so devote your time to the wine list, which is so comprehensive it could take up a rainy afternoon all by itself.

After lunch, it's time to indulge yourself. Try the Mandara Spa at the Marriott Aruba Ocean Club, which offers Swedish, sports-reflexology, and aromatherapy massages, as well as other exotic treatments, such as the exfoliating Bali Coffee Scrub. Your body will thank you. Your soul will, too. Stick around to luxuriate in the spa's mint-oil-scented steam room and pick up a pot of foot balm to carry the experience into your postvacation days. Another option is to head to the Eagle Bowling Palace, which has 16 lanes, a snack bar, and even a cocktail lounge. As you celebrate picking up that spare, you'll never know how frightful the weather is outside. Wrap up your rainy day with an early evening movie at the Seaport Cinema in the Seaport Village Market Place. Its six theaters show the latest blockbusters from Hollywood.

A PERFECT NIGHT OF ROMANCE

Aruba is one of the most romantic places on earth. Beautiful settings abound almost everywhere you look, and fine dining establishments are easy to find. Here are few hints to help rekindle your love—or maybe even start a new relationship.

Take a sunset cruise. Try a voyage on the 43-foot sailing yacht *Tranquilo*, which includes drinks (but be careful not to overdo it, as dinner lies ahead). If you don't have your sea legs yet, a catamaran cruise might be more your style. Red Sail Sports offers sunset trips with drinks and music aboard the 70-foot *Rumba*. Ocean breezes and aperitifs should whet your appetite for the next item on the agenda.

Pinchos Grill & Bar is hard to beat, even on an island filled with romantic dining options. Occupying a pier just outside of Oranjestad, the restaurant consists of a huge wooden bar surrounded by candlelit tables and comfy throw cushions. Start with a cocktail, then enjoy a lovely grilled meal prepared in front of you at the bar. The atmosphere may inspire you to linger after your meal, so relax and order dessert.

After dinner, head for the Sirocco Lounge in the Wyndham's Casablanca Casino. Sip a cocktail and listen to live jazz (Thursday through Saturday), or be daring and puff on an authentic Arabian hookah pipe. Later, test your luck at the roulette wheel. Try numbers that have special meaning for you, such as each other's birthday, your wedding anniversary, or the day you met. End the evening with a walk—hand in hand—along the beach.

A PERFECT ALL-NIGHTER

Want to take advantage of everything Aruba has to offer? Here's an action-packed guide to things to do from sundown to sunup.

Check out the Sunset Salute, accompanied by live music, at the Radisson Aruba Caribbean Resort's Sunset Bar. If you want to dance like the locals, stick around for the merengue lessons.

Papiamento Restaurant is an Aruba institution and one of the most delightful dining experiences on the island. Be sure to sit in the courtyard under the illuminated trees. The sizzling stone menu offerings are fun, but remember that the food continues to cook while on the stone—so if you like your steak rare or your seafood tender, take it off quickly. The staff are attentive and the food portions are huge; think twice before ordering an appetizer. But save room for the chocolate cake, which is nothing short of superb.

At 9 PM Monday through Saturday, check out *Let's Go Latin*—a dazzling revue of singing and dancing—at the Renaissance's Crystal Theater. Afterward, head to the trendy Garufa Cigar & Cocktail Lounge for live jazz, a cognac, and perhaps a stogie. The chic bar stools are so comfortable you may not want to leave.

The dance floor keeps getting hotter at the next stop, Mambo Jambo, well into the night. If you want to stick with Latin, head over to Cuba's Cookin'. This cozy little hideaway features live music every night and is normally packed with people belting back mojitos and enjoying the vibe.

When you just can't dance any longer, head for the 24-hour Crystal Casino, where you can give your feet a break and put on your thinking cap at the blackjack table.

By sunrise, you should be on the beach—any beach. Afterward, sip coffee, scan the local papers (or download international ones), and sink your toes into the sand at MooMba Beach Bar & Restaurant (between the Holiday Inn and the Marriott Surf Club), where you can people-watch over breakfast, beginning at 8 AM.

The couple sitting at a front table in the restaurant looks perplexed. They arrived on the morning flight and are now contemplating their first dinner on the island. They study the wide-ranging menu and look around the room as if seeking inspiration from the paintings on the wall. When the waiter arrives, they ask him for a good local choice. He suggests the keshi yena, *and the couple agrees. Moments later their meal arrives. After studying it for a few moments, they dig in. An instant later, they're all smiles as they savor the meat-and-Gouda dish. Their first Aruban culinary adventure is behind them—there's no stopping them now.*

In This Chapter

eating out

THERE ARE A FEW HUNDRED RESTAURANTS ON ARUBA, from elegant eateries to seafront shacks, so you're bound to find something to tantalize your taste buds. You can sample a wide range of cuisines—Italian, French, Argentine, Asian, and Cuban, to name a few—reflecting Aruba's eclectic blend of cultures. Chefs have to be creative on this tiny island, because of the limited number of locally grown ingredients: *maripampoen* (a vegetable that's often stewed with meat and potatoes), *hierba di hole* (a sweet-spicy herb used in fish soup), and *shimarucu* (a fruit similar to the cherry) are among the few.

Although most resorts offer better-than-average dining, don't be afraid to try one of the many excellent independent places. Ask locals about their favorite spots; some of the lesser-known restaurants offer food that's reasonably priced and definitely worth sampling.

Most restaurants on the western side of the island are along Palm Beach or in downtown Oranjestad, both easily accessible by taxi or bus. Some restaurants in Savaneta and San Nicolas are worth the trip; a car is the best way to get there.

To give visitors an affordable way to sample the island's eclectic cuisine, the **Aruba Gastronomic Association** (AGA; Rooi Santo 21, Noord, tel. 297/586–2161, 800/477–2896 in U.S., www.arubadining.com) has created a Dine-Around program involving more than 20 island restaurants. Here's how it works: you can buy tickets for three dinners ($109 per person), five dinners ($177), seven dinners ($245), or five breakfasts or lunches plus four dinners ($214). Dinners include an appetizer, an entrée, dessert, coffee or tea, and a service charge (except when a restaurant is a VIP member, in which case $36 will be deducted from your final bill instead). Other programs, such as gift certificates and coupons for dinners at the association's VIP member restaurants, are also available. You can buy Dine-Around tickets using the association's online order form, through travel agents, or at the De Palm Tours sales desk in many hotels. Participating restaurants change frequently; the AGA Web site has the latest information.

PRICES & DRESS

Aruba's elegant restaurants—where you might have to dress up a little (jackets for men, sundresses for women)—can be pricey. If you want to spend fewer florins, opt for the more casual spots, where being comfortable is the only dress requirement. A sweater draped over your shoulders will go a long way against the chill of air-conditioning. If you plan to eat in the open air, bring along insect repellent in case the mosquitoes get unruly.

CATEGORY	WHAT IT COSTS In U.S. Dollars
$$$$	over $30
$$$	$20–$30
$$	$12–$20
$	$8–$12
¢	under $8

Prices are per person for a main course at dinner, excluding service charges or taxes.

HOW & WHEN

To ensure you get to eat at the restaurants of your choice, make some calls when you get to the island—especially during high season—to secure reservations. If you're heading to a restaurant in Oranjestad for dinner, leave about 15 minutes earlier than you think you should; in-town traffic can become ugly once beach

Chowing Down Aruban Style

The finest restaurants require at the most only a jacket for men and a sundress for women. Still, after a day on the beach, even this might feel formal. For a truly casual bite, visit one of Aruba's ice-cream trucks or frietjes (pushcarts) for inexpensive, authentic Aruban finger food. Two worth the trip are El Rey Snack Truck near the Seaport Cinemas in Oranjestad, for freshly fried chicken, pork chops, and fries, and the Cellar Frietje in Oranjestad's Seaport Village Marketplace, for the best saté in town. Other island delicacies include the following:

BITTERBALLEN: steaming, bite-size meatballs. The long versions are served with mustard and called kroket. Locals wash down both varieties with beer.

FREKEDEL: a shredded fish dipped in egg and bread crumbs, rolled into balls, and deep fried.

FRIET OR BATATA: french fries—served in paper cones or Styrofoam cups—that can be topped with ketchup; mayo; curry, peanut, or hot sauce; onions; and more.

KESHI YENA: a baked concoction of Gouda cheese, spices, and meat or seafood in a rich brown sauce.

NASIBAL: a lump of seasoned rice in a crunchy coating.

PAN BATI: a pancake made of cornmeal, sugar, salt, and baking powder; eaten with meat, fish, or soup.

PASTECHI: deep-fried meat, cheese, potato, or seafood-filled turnovers, popular for breakfast. Smaller versions are called empanas.

RASPAO: a paper cup full of shaved ice that's drenched in tamarind, guava, or passion-fruit syrup.

ROTI: a tortilla-like wrap usually filled with chicken, seafood, or vegetable curry.

SATÉ: marinated chunks of chicken or pork on a bamboo skewer, grilled and served with spicy peanut sauce.

TOSTI: the ultimate grilled-cheese sandwich, often made with ham and pineapple or pepperoni.

hours are over. Note that on Sunday you may have a hard time finding a restaurant that's open for lunch, and that many eateries are closed for dinner on Sunday or Monday. Breakfast lovers are in luck. For quantity, check out the buffets at the Hyatt, Marriott, or Wyndham resorts or local joints such as DeliFrance.

Argentine

$$–$$$$ **EL GAUCHO ARGENTINE GRILL.** The atmosphere here leans toward bookcases filled with fake books and lots of turn-of-the-20th-century paraphernalia. It's usually packed with visitors coming to try the legendary, perfectly done 16-ounce steaks and decadent desserts, which can make it feel crowded at times. Massive plates can be a bit of a nuisance on the smallish tables. If you're waiting for your dinner reservation, wander over to the Garufa Lounge (same owners) for an aperitif; you will be issued with a pager that will buzz you when your table is ready. *Wilhelminastraat 80, Oranjestad, tel. 297/582–3677. www.elgaucho-aruba.com. AE, D, MC, V. Closed Sun.*

Asian

$$–$$$ **KOWLOON.** Don't be put off by the dull exterior of this fine Asian establishment. The interior decor is tasteful and relaxing, and the combination of Indonesian and authentic Chinese is truly inspired. The most interesting items are in the *Epicurean Tour of China* section of the menu. The *Setju Hoi Sin* (the house specialty), a combination of seafood, green pepper, and black bean, is a fiery but satisfying experience. *Emmastraat 11, Oranjestad, tel. 297/582–4950. www.kowloonaruba.com. AE, MC, V.*

Café

$$–$$$$ **MOOMBA BEACH BAR & RESTAURANT.** Drop by anytime—this festive eatery serves breakfast, lunch, and dinner, and the menu includes a wide selection of seafood and meat specialties. By day, sit beneath the giant *palapa* (palm-covered enclosure) if you

want to beat the heat, or plant yourself at a table in the sand if you haven't had enough sun. MooMba is popular with locals, so you can learn a bit about Aruban culture over sunset cocktails. Once a month, the place is rollicking after hours with a full-moon dance party that lures all the island's night owls. It's conveniently located on Palm Beach between the Marriott Surf Club and the Holiday Inn. The restaurant participates in AGA's Dine-Around program. *J. E. Irausquin Blvd. 230, Palm Beach, tel. 297/586–5365. www.moombabeach.com.* AE, MC, V.

Caribbean

$$–$$$$ ★ **BRISAS DEL MAR.** Many swear that this homey establishment serves the best seafood on the island. The patio setting is unbeatable, with a glorious ocean view that is especially lovely at sunset. The emphasis here is on the ingredients, rather than overly imaginative presentations. Those looking to get a taste of local favorites should try the Aruban Sensation, a selection of tasty treats that includes *keri keri* (flaked fish cooked with annatto). Service can be erratic depending on the volume of customers, and getting here can be a bit confusing, as the restaurant is located in the suburb of Savaneta. *Savaneta 222A, Savaneta, tel. 297/584–7718.* AE, D, MC, V. *Closed Mon.*

$$–$$$$ **DRIFTWOOD.** Charming owner Francine Merryweather greets you at the door of this Aruban restaurant, which resembles a series of fishermen's huts. Her husband Herby sets out on his boat every morning and brings the freshest ingredients back to the kitchen. Order his catch prepared as you like (Aruban style—panfried with a fresh tomato, vegetable, and local herbs—is best) or another of the fine fish dishes. You can't go wrong with the white sangria punch; the maître d' may even let you take home the recipe. This restaurant participates in AGA's Dine-Around program. *Klipstraat 12, Oranjestad, tel. 297/583–2515. www.driftwoodaruba.com.* MC, V. *Closed Tues.*

$$–$$$$ ★ **GASPARITO RESTAURANT & ART GALLERY.** You'll find this enchanting hideaway in a *cunucu* (country) house in Noord, not

dining

Amazonia Churrascaria, **18**

Aqua Grill, **19**

Brisas del Mar, **31**

Buccaneer, **26**

Captain's Table, **15**

Charlie's Restaurant & Bar, **33**

Chez Mathilde, **1**

Coco Plum, **2**

Cuba's Cookin', **3**

DeliFrance, **13**

Driftwood, **4**

Le Dôme, **16**

Flying Fishbone, **32**

French Steakhouse, **14**

Gasparito Restaurant & Art Gallery, **27**

El Gaucho Argentine Grill, **5**

Hostaria Da'Vittorio, **20**

Kowloon, **6**

Laguna Fish Market, **21**

L.G. Smith Steak & Chop House, **7**

Madame Janette's, **28**

Mangos, **17**

Marandi, **8**

MooMba Beach Bar & Restaurant, **22**

Old Cunucu House, **25**

Papiamento, **29**

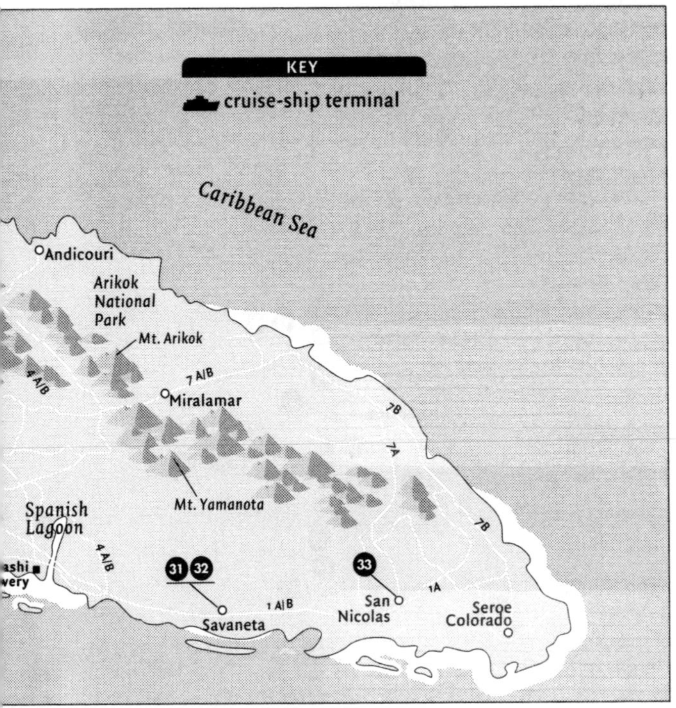

Pinchos Grill & Bar, **9**

Qué Pasa? **10**

Ruinas Del Mar, **23**

Rumba Bar & Grill, **11**

Tuscany, **24**

Ventanas del Mar, **30**

Waterfront Crabhouse, **12**

western aruba dining

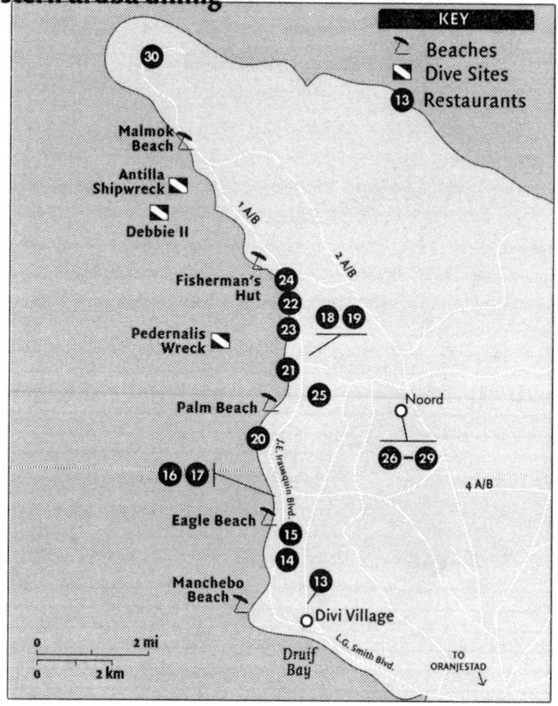

Amazonia Churrascaria, 18

Aqua Grill, 19

Buccaneer, 26

Captain's Table, 15

DeliFrance, 13

Le Dôme, 16

French Steakhouse, 14

Gasparito Restaurant & Art Gallery, 27

Hostaria Da'Vittorio, 20

Laguna Fish Market, 21

Madame Janette's, 28

Mangos, 17

MooMba Beach Bar & Restaurant, 22

Old Cunucu House, 25

Papiamento, 29

Ruinas Del Mar, 23

Tuscany, 24

Ventanas del Mar, 30

far from the hotels. Dine indoors, where works by local artists are showcased on softly lighted walls, or on the outdoor patio. Either way, the service is excellent. Order the Aruban Combo if you'd like to sample some of the island's tasty specialties, such as *keshi yena* (a dish made with Gouda and spiced meat) and stewed goat. The standout dish is the Gasparito chicken; the sauce was passed down from the owner's ancestors and features seven special ingredients, including brandy, white wine, and pineapple juice. (The rest, they say, are secret.) The restaurant participates in AGA's Dine-Around program. *Gasparito 3, Noord, tel. 297/586–7044. AE, D, MC, V. Closed Sun. No lunch.*

$$–$$$$ OLD CUNUCU HOUSE. Since the mid-1990s, executive chef Ligia Maria has delighted diners with delicious homemade meals, securing her reputation as one of Aruba's finest chefs. Try the *keshi yena* or the broiled Caribbean lobster tail served with thermidor cream sauce and topped with Parmesan cheese. For dessert, indulge in Spanish coffee with Tia Maria and brandy. Friday night features live entertainment, and on Saturday night you can have all the fajitas you can eat. *Palm Beach 150, Noord, tel. 297/586–1666. AE, D, MC, V. No lunch.*

Contemporary

$$–$$$ ★ PINCHOS GRILL & BAR. Husband-and-wife team Anabela and Robby Peterson built their restaurant on a pier just outside of Oranjestad, and it would be hard to imagine a prettier or more romantic setting. At night, hundreds of tiny lights make Pinchos glisten like a jewel in the ocean. The dining area rings the deck, so the ocean is never more than a few inches away. The huge wooden bar, which serves delicious cocktails, is a staging point for Robby to prepare his assortment of grilled specialties. He transforms ordinary ingredients into special treats; imaginative creations like mango margarita shrimp leap to life with the addition of his tequila sauce. After dinner, relax on one of the bar swings or lounge on one of the throw cushions strewn about the deck. *Surfside Marina, L.G. Smith Blvd. 7, Oranjestad, tel. 297/593–4043.*

Some Like It Hot!

Arubans like their food spicy, and that's where the island's famous Madame Janette sauce comes in handy. It's made with Scotch bonnet peppers (similar to habanero peppers), which are so hot they can burn your skin when they're broken open. Whether they're turned into pika, a relish-like mixture made with papaya, or sliced thin into vinegar and onions, these peppers are sure to set your mouth ablaze. Throw even a modest amount of Madame Janette sauce into a huge pot of soup and your taste buds will tingle. (Referring to the sauce's spicy nature, Aruban men often refer to an attractive woman as a "Madame Janette.")

To tame the flames, don't go for a glass of water, as capsaicin, the compound in peppers that produces the heat, isn't water soluble. Dairy products, sweet fruits, and starchy foods such as rice and bread are the best remedies.

$$–$$$ **RUMBA BAR & GRILL.** There's always a crowd at this lively eatery located in the heart of the downtown area. The outdoor terrace is a fun place to have a cocktail and watch the ebb and flow of Oranjestad. Deep red walls and an open kitchen featuring a charcoal grill create an inviting experience. Entrées are towering creations nestled on beds of fresh vegetables. This restaurant participates in AGA's Dine-Around program. *Havenstraat 4, Oranjestad, tel. 297/588–7900. www.rumba-aruba.com. AE, D, MC, V. Closed Sun. No lunch Sat.*

$–$$$ **MANGOS.** Hotel restaurants are often stuffy affairs, but this is not the case at Amsterdam Manor. There are no walls here to obscure the view of Eagle Beach, and the food is lovingly prepared with little fussiness. The creative world menu and relaxed atmosphere attract people from around the island, and Friday night features the popular Aruban buffet, complete with a live folkloric dance show. *Amsterdam Manor, J.E. Irausquin Blvd. 252, Eagle Beach, tel. 297/ 587–1492. AE, D, MC, V.*

Continental

$$$–$$$$ **RUINAS DEL MAR.** Local-limestone walls, lush gardens, and falling water make this one of the most stylish restaurants on the island. Chef Miguel Garcia creates memorable dishes that help complete the romantic picture. If possible, try and get a seat near the torch-lighted pond so that you can admire the black swans while dining. The Sunday champagne brunch buffet is a wonder. A 15% service charge is added to your check. *Hyatt Regency Aruba Beach Resort & Casino, J. E. Irausquin Blvd. 85, Palm Beach, tel. 297/ 586–1234. AE, D, DC, MC, V. No lunch.*

$$–$$$$ ★ **LE DÔME.** An Aruban institution, this Franco-Belgian restaurant has undergone a change of ownership, but standards remain impeccable. The emphasis is on an upscale dining experience, and the menu includes high-end offerings like *coquilles St. Jacque* (broiled scallops in a cream and wine sauce) and *sole meunière* (seasoned sole dusted with flour and sautéed in butter). But attention is lavished on even the simplest menu items; a salad arrives at your table looking like an impressionistic work of art. There are five dining rooms to choose from, each with its own special ambiance—the La Galerie room offers the best view of the sunset over Eagle Beach. Don't ignore the 16-page wine list. Le Dôme is an AGA VIP member. *J. E. Irausquin Blvd. 224, Eagle Beach, tel. 297/587–1517. www.ledome-aruba.com. Reservations essential. AE, D, DC, MC, V. No lunch Sat.*

Cuban

$$–$$$$ ★ **CUBA'S COOKIN'.** Tucked into an innocuous *cunucu* (country) house in the heart of downtown, this little gem is a hotbed of great food and fun. Locals come here for the authentic ethnic cuisine and nightly entertainment. The interior is small, so it always seems busy. Their legendary *mojitos*, a tasty mixture of light rum,

sugar, mint, and soda, pack quite a punch. *Ropa vieja* ("old clothes")—sautéed skirt steak—is a menu favorite, as is the lobster enchilada. The restaurant participates in the AGA Dine-Around program. *Wilhelminastraat 27, Oranjestad, tel. 297/588–0627. AE, MC, V.*

Eclectic

$$$–$$$$ ★ **PAPIAMENTO.** The Ellis family has been serving elegant meals in their 19th century home for almost two decades. The indoor dining room is cozy, but most diners choose to sit under the illuminated trees in the courtyard. The menu features a variety of French-inspired dishes and a healthy dose of Aruban panache. The "clay pot" seafood medley (which is broken open at the table) is a favorite, as are the "hot stone" dishes, which make for a sizzling spectacle. Be warned that the appetizer portions are larger than some restaurants' main courses. *Washington 61, Noord, tel. 297/586–4544. Reservations essential. AE, D, MC, V. No lunch. Closed Mon.*

$$$–$$$$ **VENTANAS DEL MAR.** Wall-to-wall windows allow panoramic views of the Tierra del Sol golf course and the island's western coastline. Potted palms and gold drapery complement the crisp white tablecloths in the dining room. Catering to the après-golf crowd, the menu includes a small selection of excellent entrées. Dinner features such delights as a 2-pound whole snapper fried to crispy perfection. The lunchtime menu takes a decidedly more basic approach with burgers and salads offered at upscale prices. This restaurant is an AGA VIP member. *Tierra del Sol Golf Course, Malmokweg, tel. 297/586–7800. AE, D, DC, MC, V. Closed Mon. Apr.–Nov.*

$$–$$$$ **MADAME JANETTE'S.** Named after a local chili pepper, this restaurant seems haunted by the spirit of Auguste Escoffier. Miniature portions and light sauces are well represented, and hollandaise and cheese sauces abound. Presentation is an essential part of the dining experience here, and entrées rise majestically off their plates. The best part is that everything tastes as good as it looks. Try the lamb or beef rotisseries with one of the special

sauces; if you're in the mood for something lighter, there are tasty salads. For an overwhelming finish, top off your meal with a sundae that billows over the edges of a massive champagne glass. Savor each course in the outdoor pebble garden, where tabletop candles cast a soft glow. *Cunucu Abao 37, Cunucu Abao, tel. 297/587–0184. www.madamejanette.arubahost.com. AE, MC, V. Closed Tues. No lunch.*

$$–$$$ **BUCCANEER.** Restaurants that feature a prominent theme to attract customers are not usually palaces of fine dining. Buccaneer has been drawing tourists in droves for over 20 years, and lines are par for the course during high season. The hook here is the sunken ship atmosphere—complete with a 5,000-gallon aquarium. The restaurant's main focus is seafood, but once the novelty of the decor has worn off, it becomes obvious that the food is comparable to an average North American seafood chain. The constant din of noisy children attests to the nautical setting's kiddie appeal. The restaurant participates in AGA's Dine-Around program. *Gasparito 11-C, Noord, tel. 297/586–6172. AE, D, MC, V. No lunch. Closed Sun.*

$$–$$$ **CAPTAIN'S TABLE.** The nautical surroundings might prompt you to try the cioppino, an Italian-style seafood stew, but the eclectic menu offers all sorts of other choices. Nightly piano music and a top-flight crew make for an all-around very pleasant dining experience. It's tough to choose from the extensive list of desserts, including no fewer than five options in the "death by chocolate" section. *La Cabana All Suite Beach Resort & Casino, J. E. Irausquin Blvd. 250, Eagle Beach, tel. 297/587–9000. AE, D, DC, MC, V.*

$$–$$$ **CHARLIE'S RESTAURANT & BAR.** Charlie's has been a San Nicolas hangout for more than 50 years. The walls and ceiling are *covered* with license plates, hard hats, sombreros, life preservers, baseball pennants, intimate apparel—you name it. The draw here is the nonstop party atmosphere—somewhere between a frat house and a beach bar. Decent but somewhat overpriced specialties are tenderloin and "shrimps jumbo and dumbo" (dumb because they were caught). And don't leave before sampling Charlie's "honeymoon sauce" (so called because it's really hot). *Zeppenfeldstraat 56, San Nicolas, tel. 297/584–5086. AE, D, MC, V. Closed Sun.*

$$–$$$ **LAGUNA FISH MARKET.** Louvered plantation-style doors frame the view at this colorful restaurant. You can dine inside in air-cooled comfort or outside on the terrace overlooking the lagoon. The dinner menu includes a variety of seafood choices as well as diverse items like stir-fry and sushi. The service can be a bit erratic during dinner, but the breakfast buffet is good and reasonably priced. *Radisson Aruba Resort & Casino, J. E. Irausquin Blvd. 81, Palm Beach, tel. 297/586–6555. AE, D, DC, MC, V. No lunch.*

$$–$$$ **MARANDI.** With a name that means "on the water" in Malaysian, this seaside restaurant is at once cozy and chic. Everything is seductive, from the tables tucked under a giant *palapa* (thatched structure made from palm fronds) by the water's edge to the dining room that's unencumbered by a ceiling. There are even couches set in a sandbox where you can enjoy a cocktail before your meal. The small menu offers a reasonable selection, including satisfying sushi-style tuna wrapped in seaweed and cooked tempura style. Reservations are essential for the special chef's table, where you dine right in the kitchen. *L. G. Smith Blvd. 1, Oranjestad, tel. 297/582–0157. www.marandiaruba.com. MC, V. No lunch. Closed Mon.*

$$–$$$ **QUÉ PASA?** A sign on the wall at the bar welcomes you with a friendly WHAT'S HAPPENING? in several languages. Before grabbing a table, check out the local paintings on the walls. (You might even find one to bring home.) Despite the name, there is nary a Mexican dish on the menu. Instead you'll find a selection of basic but popular items, including schnitzel and pasta. The amiable ambience on the terrace may prompt you to hang out after dinner and trade stories with the people at the next table. *Wilhelminastraat 2, Oranjestad, tel. 297/583–4888. www.quepasaaruba.com. MC, V. No lunch.*

¢–$ **COCO PLUM.** Grab a *pastechi* (meat-, cheese-, or seafood-filled turnover) and go, or stick around to relax under the thatch-roof huts and watch life unfold along Caya Betico Croes. Locals meet here for ham or tuna sandwiches, red-snapper platters, and chicken wings. Slake your thirst with an all-natural fruit drink in flavors such as watermelon, lemon, papaya, tamarind, and passion fruit. At the counter, order *loempias* (egg rolls stuffed with vegetables, chicken, or shrimp) or *empanas* (stuffed pockets of cornmeal). *Caya Betico Croes 100, Oranjestad, tel. 297/583–1176. No credit cards. No dinner. Closed Sun.*

¢–$ **DELIFRANCE.** If there is a breakfast haven in Aruba, this is it. Skip the usual hotel routine and head over to this popular deli for a selection freshly baked bagels and egg dishes galore. DeliFrance is also an excellent choice for lunch, where you can choose from dozens of sandwiches—fillings ranging from the comforting (ham and cheese) to the downright unusual (steak tartare). Save room for one of the hearty desserts, such as sugar waffles with whipped cream and strawberries or French apple turnover. The coffee alone is worth the trip. *Certified Mega Mall, L. G. Smith Blvd. 150, Oranjestad, tel. 297/588–6006. AE, D, MC, V. No dinner.*

French

$$$–$$$$ ★ **CHEZ MATHILDE.** Long considered an essential stop by serious food lovers, Chez Mathilde continues to provide modern French cuisine in the elegant surroundings of a 19th-century building. The formal dining area features burnished walls, antique lamps, and crisp white linens laid over magenta and cobalt silk skirtings. You'll almost expect Edith Piaf to walk in and burst into song. The garden room at the back provides a more relaxed, belle epoque feel, with high ceilings, potted palms, and wicker chairs. An imaginative spirit pervades the menu in offerings like duck breast and crusted ostrich breast served with asparagus and truffled potatoes. Presentation is top notch, and you'll appreciate soothing touches like a palate-cleansing mango sherbert served between

Yo, Ho, Ho & a Cake of Rum

When Venancio Felipe Bareno came to Aruba from Spain more than a half century ago, he probably didn't think that his family's rum cake recipe would make culinary history. Now the sweet little dessert is known around the world. His nephew, Bright Bakery owner Franklin Bareno, packages the pastry for local and international sales. The history of this island favorite is printed on the side of the box. Made with Aruban Palmeira rum, Natural Bridge Aruba's rum cake makes the perfect gift for folks back home. Available in two sizes, the vacuum-sealed cakes stay fresh for up to six months. The company is registered in the United States, so you can transport the cakes through customs.

courses. Aproned waiters provide attentive but understated service. Leave room for the outstanding desserts, such as the heady Grand Marnier soufflé, and be sure your credit cards have room to spare. The restaurant—run by descendants of the home's last inhabitant—is a VIP member of the AGA. *Havenstraat 23, Oranjestad, tel. 297/583–4968. www.chezmathilde.com. Reservations essential. AE, D, DC, MC, V. No lunch Sun.*

Italian

$$$–$$$$ **TUSCANY.** Attentive service and a delightful ambiance are the big draws here. A seemingly endless array of chandeliers provides soft lighting, and an earth-toned color palate and piano music add considerably to the soothing feel of the dining room. Try the *spannochie prima donna con capellini d'angelo* (sautéed shrimp with

prosciutto, shallots, wild mushrooms, and artichokes in a light grappa cream sauce on angel-hair pasta). Don't despair if the extensive menu doesn't feature your particular fancy—the kitchen may be up for a challenge. *Aruba Marriott Resort & Stellaris Casino, L. G. Smith Blvd. 101, Palm Beach, tel. 297/586–9000. Reservations essential. AE, DC, MC, V. No lunch.*

$$–$$$$ **HOSTARIA DA' VITTORIO.** Part of the fun at this family-oriented lunch and dinner spot is watching chef Vittorio Muscariello prepare authentic Italian regional specialties in the open kitchen. Rising above the decibel level of the crowd, the staff helps you choose wines from the extensive list and recommends portions of hot and cold antipasti, risottos, and pastas. Try the *branzino al sale* (sea bass baked in a hard salt shell). A 15% gratuity is automatically added to your bill at this VIP member of the AGA. As you leave, pick up some *limoncello* (lemon liqueur) at the gourmet shop. *L. G. Smith Blvd. 380, Palm Beach, tel. 297/586–3838. AE, MC, V.*

Seafood

$$$–$$$$ ★ **AQUA GRILL.** Aficionados flock here to enjoy a wide selection of seafood and the largest raw bar on the island. The atmosphere is casual, with a distinctly New England feel. Things can get a little noisy in the open dining room, but a few sips of wine from the extensive list should help numb the effect. Maine lobster and Alaskan king crab legs are available, but why try the usual fare when you can order the Fisherman's Pot, which is filled with everything from scallops to monkfish? The wood grill serves up great low-cal treats, such as mahimahi. The restaurant is an AGA VIP member. *J. E. Irausquin Boulevard 374, Palm Beach, tel. 297/586–5900. www.aqua-grill.com. AE, DC, MC, V. No lunch.*

$$$–$$$$ ★ **FLYING FISHBONE.** This friendly, relaxed beach restaurant is located well off the beaten path in Savaneta, so be sure to have a map in the car. You can dine with your toes in the sand or enjoy your meal on the wooden deck. The emphasis here is on fresh seafood—beautifully presented on colorful beds of vegetables—but there are good choices for landlubbers too. The shrimp, shiitake, and blue-cheese casserole is a tried and true favorite kept on the menu to keep the regulars happy. *Savaneta 344, Savaneta, tel. 297/584–2506. www.flyingfishbone.com. AE, D, DC, MC, V. No lunch. Closed Sun.*

$$–$$$ **WATERFRONT CRABHOUSE.** A massive lobster tank is the center of attention at Waterfront Crabhouse, where the plates are piled high with seafood. Cajun seasoning adds zing to a variety of simple but satisfying entrées, and a downtown location makes this a convenient spot for breakfast, lunch, and dinner. You can dine indoors or on the patio. The restaurant participates in AGA's Dine-Around program. *Seaport Village Marketplace, L. G. Smith Blvd. 9, Oranjestad, tel. 297/583–5858 or 297/583–6767. AE, D, DC, MC, V.*

Steak

$$$$ **AMAZONIA CHURRASCARIA.** Bring a hearty appetite to this prix-fixe eatery. The emphasis is on meat, but the sweeping salad bar (separately priced) allows calorie counters to indulge as well. Bare brick walls, floral displays, and colorful paintings make for an intimate dining experience. Amazonia participates in AGA's Dine-Around program. *J. E. Irausquin Blvd. 374, Palm Beach, tel. 297/586–4444. www.amazonia-aruba.com. AE, DC, MC, V. No lunch.*

$$–$$$$ **L.G. SMITH STEAK & CHOP HOUSE.** Cool modernity is the theme at this elegant restaurant, where white leather, dark wood, blue lighting, and limestone combine to create a memorable dining environment. The interior spaces all feel airy and open, whereas multi-level seating breaks the room into small, intimate areas. Steaks are cooked using ultra-high heat to seal in juices. Afterwards, relax over drinks and enjoy the nighttime view of Oranjestad. *Renaissance Aruba Resort & Casino, L.G. Smith Blvd. 82, Oranjestad, tel. 297/523–6115. Reservations essential. AE, D, DC, MC, V. Closed Sun.*

The Goods on Gouda

Each year Holland exports more than 250,000 tons of cheese to more than 100 countries, and Gouda (the Dutch pronounce it how-da) is one of the most popular. Gouda, named for the city where it's produced, travels well and gets harder, saltier, and more flavorful as it ages. There are six types of Gouda: young (at least 4 weeks old), semi-major (8 weeks old), major (4 months old), ultra-major (7 months old), old (10 months old), and vintage (more than a year old). When buying cheese in shops in Aruba, look for the control seal that confirms the name of the cheese, its country of origin, its fat content, and that it was officially inspected.

$$$ FRENCH STEAKHOUSE. You can hear someone say "ooh-la-la" whenever a sizzling steak is served. People come here from all over the island, which means the lines are often out the door. Classical music plays in the background as the friendly staff serves hearty meat entrées, fresh tuna or grouper, and even some vegetarian dishes. A five-course dinner includes a bottle of wine for a nice price. This eatery participates in AGA's Dine-Around program. *Manchebo Beach Resort, J. E. Irausquin Blvd. 55, Eagle Beach, tel. 297/582–3444. AE, DC, MC, V. No lunch.*

It was late in the day when the cruise ship docked. An agitated couple dashed into a jewelry shop and rushed to the gem counter, their shopping clock ticking. "Is anything wrong?" asked the clerk. "Well," said the woman, "our ship was delayed, and now we don't have time to buy all the things we wanted: earrings for my mother, a sarong for my sister, linens for our daughter, and a sculpture for our son." To accommodate the couple—and the 3,000 other passengers—the ship extended its stay until midnight, and most shops in town remained open.

In This Chapter

shopping

ARUBA'S SOUVENIR AND CRAFTS STORES ARE FULL of Dutch porcelains and figurines, as befits the island's heritage. Dutch cheese is a good buy (you're allowed to bring up to 10 pounds of hard cheese through U.S. customs), as are hand-embroidered linens and any products made from the native aloe-vera plant—sunburn cream, face masks, skin refreshers. Local arts and crafts run toward wood carvings and earthenware emblazoned with ARUBA: ONE HAPPY ISLAND and the like.

Although stores on the island often use the tag line DUTY-FREE, the word PRICES is usually printed underneath in much smaller letters. Cheaper rents, lower taxes, and a willingness to add smaller markups mean that Aruban prices on many luxury goods are often reasonable, but not truly duty-free. Most North Americans, who find clothing to be less expensive back home, buy perfume and jewelry; South Americans tend to shell out lots of cash on a variety of brand-name merchandise.

Island merchants are honest and pleasant. Still, if you encounter price markups, unsatisfactory service, or other shopping obstacles, call the tourist office, which will in turn contact the Aruba Merchants Association. A representative of the association will speak with the merchant on your behalf, even if the store isn't an association member.

HOW & WHEN

It's easy to spend money in Aruba. Most stores accept American currency and Aruban florins (written as "Afl") as well as credit cards and traveler's checks. Because there's no sales tax, the price you see on the tag is what you pay. (Note that although shopping is duty-free at large stores in town and at hotels, in tiny shops and studios you may have to pay the ABB, or value-added tax, of 6.5%.) Don't try to bargain in stores, where it's considered rude to haggle. At flea markets and souvenir stands, however, you might be able to strike a deal.

Stores are open Monday through Saturday from 8:30 or 9 to 6. Some stores stay open through the lunch hour (noon to 2), and many open when cruise ships are in port on Sunday and holidays. The later you shop in downtown Oranjestad, the easier it will be to find a place to park. Also, later hours mean slightly lower temperatures. In fact, the Aruba Merchants Association is one force behind the effort to have shops stay open later so that visitors who like to spend the day on the beach can shop in the cool of the evening.

AREAS & MALLS

Oranjestad's **CAYA G. F. BETICO CROES** is Aruba's chief shopping street, lined with several duty-free boutiques and jewelry stores noted for the aggressiveness of their vendors, especially on cruise-ship days. Most malls are in Oranjestad and are attractive gabled, pastel-hued re-creations of Dutch colonial architecture.

For late-night shopping, head to the **ALHAMBRA CASINO SHOPPING ARCADE** (L. G. Smith Blvd. 47, Manchebo Beach), open 5 PM to midnight. Souvenir shops, boutiques, and fast-food outlets fill the arcade, which is attached to the popular casino. Although small, the **AQUARIUS MALL** (Elleboogstraat 1, Oranjestad) has some upscale shops.

If you blink, you might miss the good finds at **DUTCH CROWN CENTER** (L. G. Smith Blvd. 150 [some shops face Havenstraat], Oranjestad), a tiny complex tucked between the major malls.

The **HOLLAND ARUBA MALL** (Havenstraat 6, Oranjestad) houses a collection of smart shops and eateries.

Stores at the **PORT OF CALL MARKETPLACE** (L. G. Smith Blvd. 17, Oranjestad) sell fine jewelry, perfumes, duty-free liquor, batiks, crystal, leather goods, and fashionable clothing. The **ROYAL** ★ **PLAZA MALL** (L. G. Smith Blvd. 94, Oranjestad), across from the cruise-ship terminal, has cafés, a post office (open weekdays 8–3:30), and such stores as Nautica, Benetton, Tommy Hilfiger, and Gandelman Jewelers. This is where you'll find the Cyber Café, where you can send e-mail and get your caffeine fix all in one stop.

Five minutes from the cruise-ship terminal, the **SEAPORT VILLAGE MALL** (L. G. Smith Blvd. 82, Oranjestad) is home to the Crystal Casino. More than 120 stores sell merchandise to meet every taste and budget. The pastel-hued **STRADA I AND STRADA II** (Klipstraat and Rifstraat, Oranjestad) are shopping complexes in Dutch-style buildings.

SPECIALTY ITEMS

Cigars

You'll find fine cigars at **LA CASA DEL HABANO** (Royal Plaza Mall, L. G. Smith Blvd. 94, Oranjestad, tel. 297/583–8509). At the **CIGAR EMPORIUM** (Seaport Village Mall, L. G. Smith Blvd. 82, Oranjestad, tel. 297/582–5479), the Cubans come straight from the climate-controlled humidor. Choose from Cohiba, Montecristo, Romeo y Julieta, Partagas, and more. **SUPERIOR TOBACCO** (L. G. Smith Blvd. 120, Oranjestad, tel. 297/582–3220) is a good place to shop for stogies.

Clothes

★ If you're in the mood to splurge, **AGATHA BOUTIQUE** (Seaport Village Mall, L. G. Smith Blvd. 82, Oranjestad, tel. 297/583–7965) has some high-style outfits (some up to size 18), shoes, and bags

Ronchi de Cuba's Aruban Style

"Shopping has recently become tremendously advanced on Aruba," says local fashion designer Ronchi de Cuba. "We're seeing higher-end fashion that's more reasonably priced, from companies like Fendi and Gucci, and the shopping area is still growing." He says the best time to get great buys at the high-end stores is in January, when the holidays are over and the racks are being cleared for the new season.

De Cuba became involved in fashion at age 17, thanks to a high school physical-education assignment for which he taught a dance class and presented a show that incorporated theater, choreography, and fashion. After attending college in Miami, de Cuba returned to his native Aruba to work at a modeling agency. Soon after, he opened his own agency to promote local entertainment and style.

The first Ronchi de Cuba design was a haute-couture number created for Miss Aruba 1999; he has since gone on to create ready-to-wear swimwear, menswear, women's wear, and junior lines. When he's not cutting clothes, the designer travels to New York, Miami, and Paris to peek into the shops and showrooms of major designers.

De Cuba clothes are constructed of fabrics suitable for a warm climate: crepe linens, silk georgettes, and shantungs for day; brocade, wool crepe, crepe de chine, and silk chiffon for evening. Inspired by such designers as John Galliano, Dolce & Gabbana, and Prada, his collections feature playful color schemes that incorporate dark solids, bright colors, and prints. He turns out a spring-summer collection and a holiday-cruise collection each year.

Always on the cutting edge of fashion, de Cuba is also known on the island for hosting the annual International Male Model contest, featuring dozens of contestants from the Caribbean, South and Central America, the United States, the United Arab Emirates, and Europe.

Look for de Cuba's label at stores in the Seaport Village Marketplace and the Royal Plaza Mall or at his own shop—Revolution—in Oranjestad.

by New York fashion designer Agatha Brown. Sample at least one of her two signature fragrances, derived from floral and citrus scents.

People come to **CAPERUCITA RAJA** (Wilhelminastraat 17, Oranjestad, tel. 297/583–6166) for designer baby, children's, and junior clothes, as well as a wide selection of shoes. Outfits that cost $21 here sell for more than three times that amount at Saks Fifth Avenue. Forget to pack your intimates? **COLOMBIA MODA** (Wilhelminastraat 19, Oranjestad, tel. 297/582–3460) will help complete your wardrobe with lingerie made of high-quality microfiber fabrics. **CONFETTI** (Seaport Village Mall, L. G. Smith Blvd. 82, Oranjestad, tel. 297/583–8614) has the hottest European and American swimsuits, cover-ups, and other beach essentials.

★ **DEL SOL** (Royal Plaza Mall, L. G. Smith Blvd. 94, Oranjestad, tel. 297/583–8448) is the place to buy beach accessories such as sun visors, and shirts and shorts that change colors in the sun. **EXTREME SPORTS** (Royal Plaza Mall, L. G. Smith Blvd. 94, Oranjestad, tel. 297/583–8458) sells everything sportsaholics could ever need. Invest in a set of in-line skates or a boogie board, or pick up a backpack, bathing suit, or pair of reef walkers in funky shades. A venerated name in Aruba, **J. L. PENHA & SONS** (Caya G. F. Betico Croes 11/13, Oranjestad, tel. 297/582–4160 or 297/582–4161) sells high-end perfumes and cosmetics. It stocks such brands as Boucheron, Cartier, Dior, and Givenchy.

At **MANGO** (Main St. 9, Oranjestad, tel. 297/582–9700)—part of an international chain—you'll find fashions from as far away as Spain. **MODA ACTUAL** (Caya G. F. Betico Croes 49, Oranjestad, tel. 297/583–1202) rotates its reasonably priced, high-quality merchandise about every two months. Popular items include preshrunk cotton tank tops and T-shirts for men and women. If the Aruban sun doesn't make your life sizzle, the sexy lingerie at **SECRETS OF ARUBA** (Seaport Village Mall, L. G. Smith Blvd. 82,

Oranjestad, tel. 297/583–0897) just might. The store also sells oils and lotions that aren't used for getting a tan. As the many repeat customers will tell you, **SUN + SAND** (Dutch Crown Center, L. G. Smith Blvd. 150, Oranjestad, tel. 297/583–8812) is *the* place for T-shirts, sweatshirts, polo shirts, and cover-ups.

For innovative activewear, check out **TOMMY HILFIGER** (Royal Plaza Mall, L. G. Smith Blvd. 94, Oranjestad, tel. 297/583–8548). Be sure to visit the Tommy Jeans store as well. Menswear reigns supreme at **LA VENEZOLANA** (Steenweg 12, Oranjestad, tel. 297/582–1444). You'll find blazers and suits as well as jeans, belts, and shoes. Look for such names as Givenchy, Lee Jeans, and Van Heusen.

★ **WULFSEN & WULFSEN** (Caya G. F. Betico Croes 52, Oranjestad, tel. 297/582–3823) has been one of the most highly regarded clothing stores in Aruba and the Netherlands Antilles for 30 years. It carries elegant suits for men and linen cocktail dresses for women, and it's also a great place to buy bathing suits and Bermuda shorts.

Food

The clean, orderly **KONG HING SUPERMARKET** (L. G. Smith Blvd. 152, Bushiri, tel. 297/582–5545) stocks all the comforts of home—from fresh cuts of meat to prepackaged salads to Lean Cuisine dinners. The liquor section offers everything from exotic liqueurs to familiar beers. There's also a pharmacy with name-brand items such as Goody hair supplies and Bausch & Lomb eye-care products. The market, which is open Monday to Saturday 8 to 8 and Sunday 9 to 1, accepts Discover, MasterCard, and Visa for purchases of $10 or more. There's also an ATM on the premises.

The family-owned and -operated **LING & SONS SUPERMARKET** (Italiëstraat 26, Eagle Beach, tel. 297/583–2370, www.visitaruba.com/ling&sons) is one of the island's top grocers. In addition to a wide variety of foods, there's a bakery, a deli, a butcher shop, and a well-stocked "liquortique." If you e-mail ahead, the store can have a package of essential foodstuffs delivered to your hotel room in time for your arrival. The market is open Monday to Saturday 8 to 8 and Sunday 9 to 1. Before the December holidays, the store sometimes stays open an hour later on weekdays.

Gifts & Souvenirs

★ **ART & TRADITION HANDICRAFTS** (Caya G. F. Betico Croes 30, Oranjestad, tel. 297/583–6534; Royal Plaza Mall, L. G. Smith Blvd. 94, Oranjestad, tel. 297/582–7862) sells intriguing souvenirs. Buds from the *mopa mopa* tree are boiled to form a resin colored by vegetable dyes. Artists then stretch the resin by hand and mouth, and tiny pieces are cut and layered to form intricate designs—and truly unusual gifts.

The **ARTISTIC BOUTIQUE** (Caya G. F. Betico Croes 25, Oranjestad, tel. 297/582–3142; Wyndham Aruba Beach Resort & Casino, J. E. Irausquin Blvd. 77, tel. 297/586–4466 Ext. 3508; Seaport Village Mall, L. G. Smith Blvd. 82, Oranjestad, tel. 297/583–2567; Holiday Inn Sunspree Aruba Beach Resort & Casino, J. E. Irausquin Blvd. 230, tel. 297/583–3383) has been in business for more than 30 years. It's known for its Giuseppe Armani figurines from Italy, usually sold at a 20% discount; Aruban hand-embroidered linens; gold and silver jewelry; and porcelain and pottery from Spain.

EL BOHIO (Port of Call Marketplace, L. G. Smith Blvd. 17, Oranjestad, tel. 297/582–9178) will charm you with its wooden-hut displays holding Arawak-style pottery, Dutch shoes, and wind chimes. You'll also find classic leather handbags. **CREATIVE HANDS** (Socotorolaan 5, Oranjestad, tel. 297/583–5665) sells porcelain and ceramic miniatures of *cunucu* (country) houses and divi-divi trees, but the store's real draw is its exquisite Japanese dolls. For pottery lovers, **KWA KWA** (Port of

Call Marketplace, L. G. Smith Blvd. 17, Oranjestad, tel. 297/583–9471) is a paradise. There are wind chimes, pottery, and knickknacks galore—all made of ceramic, of course. Other items include embroidered bags.

While you wait 30 minutes for your film to be developed or your digital images to be printed at **NEW FACE PHOTO** (Dutch Crown Center, Havenstraat 27, Oranjestad, tel. 297/582–9510), you can shop for gifts. At **VIBES** (Royal Plaza Mall, L. G. Smith Blvd. 93, Oranjestad, tel. 297/583–7949), treat yourself to a Monte Crisco or Cohiba cigar, and pick up souvenirs such as postcards, picture frames, and T-shirts. Clothes from Aruba and Indonesia, hand-painted mobiles, and bamboo wind chimes are among the goodies at **TROPICAL WAVE** (Port of Call Marketplace, L. G. Smith Blvd. 17, Oranjestad, tel. 297/582–1905).

Housewares

Locals swear by **DECOR HOME FASHIONS** (Steenweg 14, Oranjestad, tel. 297/582–6620), which sells sheets, towels, place mats, and other linens imported from Italy, Germany, Holland, Portugal, and the United States.

Jewelry

Filling 6,000 square feet of space, **BOOLCHAND'S** (Seaport Village Mall, L. G. Smith Blvd. 82, Oranjestad, tel. 297/583–0147) sells jewelry and watches. It also stocks leather goods, cameras, and electronics. If green fire is your passion, **COLOMBIAN EMERALDS** (Seaport Village Mall, L. G. Smith Blvd. 82, Oranjestad, tel. 297/583–6238) has a dazzling array. There are also fine watches by Raymond Weil, Baume & Mercier, Jaeger-Le Coultre, Ebel, Seiko, Citizen, and Tissot. For all that glitters, head to **DIAMONDS INTERNATIONAL** (Port of Call Marketplace, L. G. Smith Blvd. 17, Oranjestad, tel. 800/515–3935). **GANDELMAN JEWELERS** (Royal Plaza Mall, L. G. Smith Blvd. 94, Oranjestad, tel. 297/583–4433) sells Gucci and Rolex watches at reasonable prices. The store also has gold bracelets and a full line of Lladro figurines. Find one-of-a-kind silver pieces ★ at **GRACE SILVER & BEYOND** (Seaport Marketplace 13, L. G. Smith Blvd. 9, Oranjestad, tel. 297/588–6262). **KENRO JEWELERS** (Seaport Village Mall, L. G. Smith Blvd. 82, Oranjestad, tel. 297/583–4847 or 297/583–3171) has two stores in the same mall, attesting to the popularity of its stock of bracelets and necklaces from Ramon Leopard; jewelry by Arando, Micheletto, and Blumei; and various brands of watches. There are also six other locations, including some in the major hotels.

Precious pearls add lustre to many of the pretty items at **PEARL GEMS FINE JEWELRY** (L. G. Smith Blvd. 90-92, Oranjestad, tel. 297/588–4927).

Leather Goods

ALIVIO (Steenweg 12-1, Oranjestad) has shoes for men, women, and children. Whether you're walking around town by day or dressing up for dinner at night, you'll find something suitable in this Oranjestad shop. Look for Birkenstock from Germany, Piedro and Wolky from Holland, and Mephisto from France.

If you get lucky, you'll catch one of the year's big sales (one is held the first week in December, the other the first week in February) at **GUCCI** (Seaport Village Mall, L. G. Smith Blvd. 82, Oranjestad, tel. 297/583–3952), when prices are slashed on handbags, luggage, wallets, shoes, watches, belts, and ties. **FERRAGAMO** (Emmastraat 1, Oranjestad, tel. 297/582–8218) has a popular boutique behind Royal Plaza Mall.

Luxury Goods

For perfumes, cosmetics, men's and women's clothing, and leather goods (including Bally shoes), stop in at **ARUBA TRADING COMPANY** (Caya G. F. Betico Croes 12, Oranjestad, tel. 297/582–2602), which has been in business for nearly 75 years.

Beyond T-Shirts and Key Chains

You can't go wrong with baseball caps, refrigerator magnets, beer mugs, sweatshirts, T-shirts, key chains, and other local logo merchandise. You won't go broke buying these items, either.

BUDGET FOR A MAJOR PURCHASE If souvenirs are all about keeping the memories alive in the long haul, plan ahead to shop for something really special—a work of art, a rug or something else hand-crafted, or a major accessory for your home. One major purchase will stay with you far longer than a dozen tourist trinkets.

ADD TO YOUR COLLECTION Whether antiques, used books, salt and pepper shakers, or ceramic frogs are your thing, start looking in the first day or two. Chances are you'll want to scout around and then go back to some of the first shops you visited before you hand over your credit card.

GET GUARANTEES IN WRITING Is the vendor making promises? Ask him to put them in writing.

ANTICIPATE A SHOPPING SPREE If you think you might buy breakables, include a length of bubble wrap. Pack a large tote bag in your suitcase in case you need extra space. Don't fill your suitcase to bursting before you leave home. Or include some old clothing that you can leave behind to make room for new acquisitions.

KNOW BEFORE YOU GO Study prices at home on items you might consider buying while you're away. Otherwise you won't recognize a bargain when you see one.

PLASTIC, PLEASE Especially if your purchase is pricey and you're looking for authenticity, it's always smart to pay with a credit card. If a problem arises later and the merchant can't or won't resolve it, the credit-card company may help you out.

★ **LITTLE SWITZERLAND** (Caya G. F. Betico Croes 14, Oranjestad, tel. 297/582–1192; Royal Plaza Mall, L. G. Smith Blvd. 94, Oranjestad, tel. 297/583–4057), the St. Thomas–based giant, is the place to go for china, crystal, and fine tableware. You'll also find good buys on Omega and Rado watches, Swarovski and Baccarat crystal, and Lladro figurines.

At **WEITNAUER** (Caya G. F. Betico Croes 29, Oranjestad, tel. 297/582–2790) you'll find specialty Lenox items as well as a wide range of fragrances.

Oblivious to the casino's din, a handful of blackjack players are on the edge of their seats. Each has split his or her cards, and there's a lot of money at stake. The dealer's hand totals 16. One player wipes the sweat from his brow; another takes a long drag on her cigarette and slowly exhales. A group of onlookers whisper their predictions. With a flourish, the dealer pulls his final card—a queen! The players shout for joy.

In This Chapter

casinos

THERE WAS A TIME WHEN WOMEN DRESSED in evening gowns and men donned suits for a chic, glamorous night in Aruba's casinos. In the mid-'80s, however, the Alhambra Casino opened, touting its philosophy of "barefoot elegance." Suddenly shorts and T-shirts became acceptable attire. The relaxed dress code made gaming seem an affordable pastime rather than a luxury.

Aruba's casinos now attract high rollers, low-stakes bettors, and nongamblers alike. Games include slot machines, blackjack (both beloved by North Americans), baccarat (preferred by South Americans), craps, roulette—even betting on sports events. Theaters, restaurants, bars, and cigar shops have added another dimension to the casinos. Now you can go out for dinner, take in a show, sip after-dinner drinks, and play blackjack all under one roof. In between games, you can get to know other patrons and swap tips and tales. The many local entertainers who rotate among the casinos add to the excitement.

THE CASINOS

Except for the free-standing Alhambra, most casinos are found in hotels; all are along Palm Beach or Eagle Beach or in downtown Oranjestad. Although the minimum age to enter is 18, some venues are relaxed about this rule. By day, "barefoot elegance" is the norm in all casinos, although many establishments have a shirt-and-shoes requirement. Evening dress is expected to be more polished, though still casual. In high season, the casinos are open from just before noon to the wee hours; in low season (May to November), they may not start dealing until late afternoon.

If you plan to play large sums of money, check in with the casino upon arrival so that you'll be rewarded for your business. Most hotels offer gambling goodies—complimentary meals at local restaurants, chauffeured tours, and, in the cases of big spenders, high-roller suites. Even small-scale gamblers may be entitled to coupons for meals and discounted rooms.

★ **ALHAMBRA CASINO.** Here, amid the Spanish-style arches and leaded glass, a "Moorish slave" named Roger gives every gambler a hearty handshake upon entering. The atmosphere is casual, and with $5 tables, no one need feel intimidated. Try your luck at blackjack, Caribbean stud poker, three-card poker, roulette, craps, or one of the 300 slot machines that accept American nickels, quarters, and dollars. Head to one of the novelty touch-screen machines, each of which has a variety of games. There's also bingo every Saturday, Monday, and Thursday beginning at 1 PM. If you fill your card, you can collect the grand prize of a few hundred dollars—not bad for a $5 investment. Be sure to sign up for the Alhambra Advantage Card, which gives you a point for each dollar you spend—even if you lose at the tables, you can still go home with prizes. Of course, winners can spend their earnings immediately at the many on-site shops. The casino is owned by the Divi Divi resorts, and golf carts run to and from nearby hotels every 15 minutes or so. The slots here open daily at 10 AM; gaming tables operate from 6 PM until 4 AM. *L. G. Smith Blvd. 47, Oranjestad, tel. 297/583–5000 Ext. 480 or 482.*

ALLEGRO CASINO. Famous movie stars gaze down at you from a 30-foot mural as you take your chances at one of 245 slots or at dozens of blackjack, roulette, poker, craps, baccarat, and Caribbean stud poker tables. The casino at the Occidental

Allegro Resort opens daily at noon for slots and at 5 PM for all other games. The entire gaming floor joins in the free full-card bingo game held nightly at 10:30. Anyone who scores a full card within the first 50 calls wins a clean grand; everyone who shows a full card after that walks away with $100. There's a slot tournament every Friday at 8 PM, and look for double jackpots daily from 3 to 5 PM. You can hang around until 4 AM. *J. E. Irausquin Blvd. 83, Palm Beach, tel. 297/586–9039. www.allegroresorts.com.*

CASABLANCA CASINO. Smart money is on the Wyndham Aruba Beach Resort's quietly elegant casino, which has a Humphrey Bogart theme and a tropical color scheme. Spend some time at the blackjack, roulette, craps, stud poker, and baccarat tables, or the slot machines. Seek out the unique Feature Frenzy machines, which reportedly pay out $6,000 jackpots daily. If gambling isn't your style, visit the Sirocco Lounge for exotic cocktails and live jazz most nights at 9. Or you can take in the Aruba Carnival Havana Tropical shows. The casino is open daily from noon to 4 AM. *J. E. Irausquin Blvd. 77, Palm Beach, tel. 297/586–4466. www.wyndham.com.*

CASINO AT THE RADISSON ARUBA RESORT. Although it measures 16,000 square feet, you may have a hard time finding this casino. Descend the stairs at the corner of the resort's lobby, following the sounds of the piano player's tunes. The nightly action here includes Las Vegas–style blackjack, roulette, craps, and slot machines. Overhead, thousands of lights simulate shooting stars that seem destined to carry out your wishes for riches. A host of shops and restaurants let you chip away at your newfound wealth. The slots here open daily at noon, and the table action begins at 6 PM. Everything shuts down at 4 AM. *J. E. Irausquin Blvd. 81, Palm Beach, tel. 297/586–4045. www.radisson.com.*

★ **COPACABANA CASINO.** Ablaze with neon, the Hyatt Regency Aruba Beach Resort's ultramodern casino is an enormous complex with a Carnival-in-Rio theme. The most popular games

Good-Luck Charms

Arubans take myths and superstitions very seriously. They flinch if a black butterfly flits into their home, because this symbolizes death. They gasp if a child crawls under their legs, because it's a sign that the baby won't grow anymore. And on New Year's Eve, they toss the first sips of whiskey, rum, or champagne from the first bottle that's opened in the New Year out the door of their house to show respect to those who have died and to wish luck on others. It's no surprise, then, that good-luck charms are part of Aruba's casino culture as well.

The island's most common good-luck charm is the djucu *(pronounced* joo-koo*), a brown-and-black stone that comes from the sea and becomes hot when rubbed. Many people have them put in gold settings—with their initials engraved in the metal—and wear them around their necks on a chain with other charms such as an anchor or a cross. Another item that's thought to bring good luck is a small bag of sand. Women wear them tucked discreetly into their bras; one woman who visited Aruba every year always carried a few cloves of garlic in her bag. On a recent visit, she removed the garlic, placed it on a slot machine, and won $1,000 instantly. All the more reason to save the scraps from your salad plate when you leave dinner.*

here are slots, blackjack, craps, and baccarat. Slots and some other games are available at noon, the dice start rolling at 6 PM, and all other pursuits are open by 8 PM. From 9 PM to 2 AM, there's live music at the stage near the bar—you'll find it hard to steal away from the pulsating mix of Latin and American tunes. Don't forget to register for free dinners and brunches and hotel discounts at the hostess station. The casino is open until 4 AM. *J. E. Irausquin Blvd. 85, Palm Beach, tel. 297/586–1234. www.hyatt.com.*

★ **CRYSTAL CASINO.** Adorned with Austrian crystal chandeliers and gold-leaf columns, the Renaissance Aruba Beach Resort Marina Tower's glittering casino evokes Monaco's grand establishments—hence, the international clientele. The Salon Privé offers serious gamblers a private room for baccarat, roulette, and high-stakes blackjack. This casino is popular among cruise-ship passengers, who stroll over from the port to watch and play in slot tournaments and bet on sporting events. The Crystal Lounge, which overlooks the betting floor, serves up live music along with the cocktails, and the Crystal Theater's shows—*Let's Go Latin* and *Aruba Panorama*—are big hits on the island. *L. G. Smith Blvd. 82, Oranjestad, tel. 297/583–6000. www.arubarenaissance.com.*

EXCELSIOR CASINO. The Holiday Inn SunSpree Aruba Beach Resort's casino—the birthplace of Caribbean stud poker—has blackjack, craps, and roulette tables, plenty of slot machines, and a bar featuring live entertainment. There's also a poker room for Texas hold 'em, seven-card stud, and Caribbean stud. It's the only casino on Palm Beach with an ATM adjacent to the cashier. Afternoon bingo overtakes the main floor every weekday at 3:30 PM. The casino is open daily from 8 AM to 4 AM; slots begin spinning at 9 AM, and tables open at 12:30 PM. *J. E. Irausquin Blvd. 230, Palm Beach, tel. 297/586–3600. www.holidayinn-aruba.com.*

ROYAL CABANA CASINO. Reputedly the largest casino in the Caribbean, Royal Cabana has a sleek interior that holds 372 slot machines. The casino offers the highest-stakes bingo games around, Monday to Saturday at 1 PM and 3:30 PM. The Tropicana Showroom is known for the energy of such hit shows as *Don't Tell Mama* and *La Cage aux Folles*. The slots here open daily at 11 AM, the tables at 4 PM. The casino, next door to the La Cabana All Suite Beach Resort, closes at 4 AM. *J. E. Irausquin Blvd. 250, Eagle Beach, tel. 297/587–4665. www.lacabana.com.*

SEAPORT CASINO. The gambling is low-key at this waterside establishment adjacent to the Renaissance Aruba Beach Resort's Beach Tower, the Seaport Marketplace, and the Seaport Conference Center. More than 200 slot machines are in daily operation from 10 AM to 4 AM, and tables are open from 4 PM to 4 AM. From here, you can see the boats on the ocean and enjoy not only the games you'd find at other casinos but also shops, restaurants, bars, and movie theaters. Stop by on Tuesday, Thursday, or Sunday for the casino's popular bingo tournaments. *L. G. Smith Blvd. 9, Oranjestad, tel. 297/583–5027 Ext. 4212.*

★ **STELLARIS CASINO.** The Aruba Marriott Resort's casino has mirrors on the ceilings that reflect the glamorous chandeliers. Start at the slots at noon or the tables at 4 PM, and play until 4 AM if you're on a roll. Take your pick of craps, roulette, Caribbean stud poker, minibaccarat, and superbuck (like blackjack with suits). Every night except Sunday there's a performance by musician Cesar Olarta that may boost your luck. Check-in with the casino when you arrive at the hotel and you'll get a membership card. If you play high enough stakes at the tables, you can win free meals and other prizes. If not, you'll at least get a postcard in the mail offering a special rate on future stays. The hotel offers a 30% discount to those who play at least four hours each day. *L. G. Smith Blvd. 101, Palm Beach, tel. 297/586–9000. www.marriott.com.*

THE GAMES

For a short-form handbook on the rules, the odds, and the strategies for the most popular casino games—or for help deciding on the kind of action that suits your style—read on.

The first part of any casino strategy is to risk the most money on wagers that present the lowest edge for the house. Blackjack, craps, video poker, and baccarat are the most advantageous to the bettor. The two types of bets at baccarat have a house advantage of a little more than 1%. The basic line bets at craps, if backed up with full odds, can be as low as 0.5%. Blackjack and video poker can not only put you even with the house (a true 50-50 proposition) but give you a slight long-term advantage.

How can a casino provide you with a 50-50 or even a positive expectation at some of its games? First, because a vast number of suckers make bad bets (those with a house advantage of 5%–35%, such as roulette, keno, and slots). Second, because the casino knows that very few people are aware of the opportunities to beat the odds. Third, because it takes skill to exploit these opportunities. However, a mere hour or two spent learning strategies for the games that favor the gambler will put you ahead of most visitors, who give the gambling industry an average 12%–15% profit margin.

BACCARAT

The most "glamorous" game in the casino, baccarat is a version of *chemin de fer,* which is popular in European gambling halls. It's a favorite with high rollers because thousands of dollars are often staked on one hand. The Italian word *baccara* means "zero." This refers to the point value of 10s and picture cards. The game is run by four pit personnel. Two dealers sit side by side at the middle of the table. They handle the winning and losing bets and keep track of each player's "commission" (explained below). The caller stands in the middle of the other side of the table and dictates the action. The "ladderman" supervises the game and acts as final judge if any disputes arise.

How to Play

Baccarat is played with eight decks of cards dealt from a large "shoe" (or cardholder). Each player is offered a turn at handling the shoe and dealing the cards. Two two-card hands are dealt: the "player" and the "bank" hands. The player who deals the cards is called the banker, although the house banks both hands. The players bet on which hand—player or banker—will come closest to adding up to 9 (a "natural"). Ace through 9 retain face value, and 10s and picture cards are worth zero. If you have a hand adding up to more than 10, the number 10 is subtracted from the total. For example, if one hand contains a 10 and a 4, the hand adds up to 4. If the other holds an ace and a 6, it adds up to 7. If a hand has a 7 and a 9, it adds up to 6.

Depending on the two hands, the caller either declares a winner and loser (if either hand actually adds up to 8 or 9) or calls for another card for the player hand (if it totals 1, 2, 3, 4, 5, or 10). The bank hand then either stands pat or draws a card, determined by a complex series of rules depending on what the player's total is and dictated by the caller. When one or the other hand is declared a winner, the dealers go into action to pay off the winning wagers, collect the losing wagers, and add up the commission (usually 5%) that the house collects on the bank hand. Both bets have a house advantage of slightly more than 1%.

The player-dealer (or banker) holds the shoe as long as the bank hand wins. When the player hand wins, the shoe moves counterclockwise around the table. Players can refuse the shoe and pass it to the next player. Because the caller dictates the action, player responsibilities are minimal. It's not necessary to know the card-drawing rules, even if you're the banker.

Baccarat Strategy

To bet, you only have to place your money in the bank, player, or tie box on the layout, which appears directly in front of where you sit. If you're betting that the bank hand will win, you put your chips in the bank box; bets for the player hand go in the player box. (Only real suckers bet on the tie.) Most players bet on the bank hand when they deal, since they "represent" the bank and to do otherwise would seem as if they were betting "against" themselves. This isn't really true, but it seems that way. Playing baccarat is a simple matter of guessing whether the player or banker hand will come closest to 9 and deciding how much to bet on the outcome.

BLACKJACK

How to Play

You play blackjack against a dealer, and whichever of you comes closest to a card total of 21 wins. Number cards are worth their face value, picture cards are worth 10, and aces are worth either 1 or 11. (Hands with aces are known as "soft" hands. Always count the ace first as an 11. If you also have a 10, your total will be 21, not 11.) If the dealer has a 17 and you have a 16, you lose. If you have an 18 against a dealer's 17, you win (even money). If both you and the dealer have a 17, it's a tie (or "push") and no money changes hands. If you go over a total of 21 (or "bust"), you lose, even if the dealer also busts later in the hand. If your first two cards add up to 21 (a "natural"), you're paid 3 to 2. However, if the dealer also has a natural, it's a push. A natural beats a total of 21 achieved with more than two cards.

You're dealt two cards, either facedown or faceup, depending on the custom of the casino. The dealer also gives herself two cards, one facedown and one faceup (except in double-exposure blackjack, where both the dealer's cards are visible). Depending on your first two cards and the dealer's up card, you can **STAND,** or refuse to take another card. You can **HIT,** or take as many cards as you need until you stand or bust. You can **DOUBLE DOWN,** or double your bet and take one card. You can **SPLIT** a like pair; if you're dealt two 8s, for example, you can double your bet and play the 8s as if they're two hands. You can **BUY INSURANCE** if the dealer is showing an ace. Here you're wagering half your initial bet that the dealer *does* have a natural. If so, you lose your initial bet but are paid 2 to 1 on the insurance (which means the whole thing is a push). You can **SURRENDER** half your initial bet if you're holding a bad hand (known as a "stiff") such as a 15 or 16 against a high-up card such as a 9 or 10.

Blackjack Strategy

Many people devote a great deal of time to learning complicated statistical schemes. However, if you don't have the time, energy, or inclination to get that seriously involved, the following basic strategies should allow you to play the game with a modicum of skill and a paucity of humiliation:

When your hand is a stiff (a total of 12, 13, 14, 15, or 16) and the dealer shows a 2, 3, 4, 5, or 6, always stand.

When your hand is a stiff and the dealer shows a 7, 8, 9, 10, or ace, always hit.

When you hold 17, 18, 19, or 20, always stand.

When you hold a 10 or 11 and the dealer shows a 2, 3, 4, 5, 6, 7, 8, or 9, always double down.

When you hold a pair of aces or a pair of 8s, always split.

Never buy insurance.

CRAPS

Craps is a dice game played at a large rectangular table with rounded corners. Up to 12 players can stand around the table.

The layout is mounted at the bottom of a surrounding rail, which prevents the dice from being thrown off the table and provides an opposite wall against which to bounce the dice. It can require up to four pit personnel to run an action-packed, fast-paced game of craps. Two dealers handle the bets made on either side of the layout. A "stickman" wields the long wooden stick, curved at one end, which is used to move the dice around the table. The stickman also calls the number that's rolled and books the proposition bets made in the middle of the layout. The "boxman" sits between the two dealers, overseeing the game and settling any disputes.

How to Play

Stand at the table wherever you can find an open space. You can start betting casino chips immediately, but you have to wait your turn to be the shooter. The dice are passed clockwise around the table (the stickman will give you the dice at the appropriate time). It's important, when you're the shooter, to roll the dice hard enough so they bounce off the end wall of the table. This shows that you're not trying to control the dice with a "soft roll."

Craps Strategy

Playing craps is fairly straightforward; it's the betting that's complicated. The basic concepts are as follows: If the first time the shooter rolls the dice he or she turns up a 7 or 11, that's called a "natural"—an automatic win. If a 2, 3, or 12 comes up on the first throw (called the "come-out roll"), that's termed "craps"—an automatic lose. Each of the numbers 4, 5, 6, 8, 9, or 10 on a first roll is known as a "point": the shooter keeps rolling the dice until the point comes up again. If a 7 turns up before the point does, that's another loser. When either the point or a losing 7 is rolled, this is known as a "decision," which happens on average every 3.3 rolls.

But "winning" and "losing" rolls of the dice are entirely relative in this game, because there are two ways you can bet at craps: "for" the shooter or "against" the shooter. Betting for means that the shooter will "make his point" (win). Betting against means that the shooter will "seven out" (lose). Either way, you're actually betting against the house, which books all wagers. If you're betting "for" on the come-out, you place your chips on the layout's "pass line." If a 7 or 11 is rolled, you win even money. If a 2, 3, or 12 (craps) is rolled, you lose your bet. If you're betting "against" on the come-out, you place your chips in the "don't pass bar." A 7 or 11 loses; a 2, 3, or 12 wins. A shooter can bet for or against himself, or against other players.

There are also roughly two dozen wagers you can make on any single specific roll of the dice. Craps strategy books can give you the details on come/don't come, odds, place, buy, big six, field, and proposition bets.

ROULETTE

Roulette is a casino game that uses a perfectly balanced wheel with 38 numbers (0, 00, and 1 through 36), a small white ball, a large layout with 11 different betting options, and special "wheel chips." The layout organizes 11 different bets into 6 "inside bets" (the single numbers, or those closest to the dealer) and 5 "outside bets" (the grouped bets, or those closest to the players).

The dealer spins the wheel clockwise and the ball counterclockwise. When the ball slows, the dealer announces, "No more bets." The ball drops from the "back track" to the "bottom track," caroming off built-in brass barriers and bouncing in and out of the different cups in the wheel before settling into the cup of the winning number. Then the dealer places a marker on the number and scoops all the losing chips into her corner. Depending on how crowded the game is, the casino can count on roughly 50 spins of the wheel per hour.

How to Play

To buy in, place your cash on the layout near the wheel. Inform the dealer of the denomination of the individual unit you intend to play. Know the table limits (displayed on a sign in the dealer area). Don't ask for a 25¢ denomination if the minimum is $1. The dealer gives you a stack of wheel chips of a color that is different from those of all the other players and places a chip marker atop one of your wheel chips on the rim of the wheel to identify its denomination. Note that you must cash in your wheel chips at the roulette table before you leave the game. Only the dealer can verify how much they're worth.

Roulette Strategy

INSIDE BETS

With inside bets, you can lay any number of chips (depending on the table limits) on a single number, 1 through 36 or 0 or 00. If the number hits, your payoff is 35 to 1, for a return of $36. You could, conceivably, place a $1 chip on all 38 numbers, but the return of $36 would leave you $2 short, which divides out to 5.26%, the house advantage. If you place a chip on the line between two numbers and one of those numbers hits, you're paid 17 to 1 for a return of $18 (again, $2 short of the true odds). Betting on three numbers returns 11 to 1, four numbers returns 8 to 1, five numbers pays 6 to 1 (this is the worst bet at roulette, with a 7.89% disadvantage), and six numbers pays 5 to 1.

OUTSIDE BETS

To place an outside bet, lay a chip on one of three "columns" at the lower end of the layout next to numbers 34, 35, and 36. This pays 2 to 1. A bet placed in the first 12, second 12, or third 12 boxes also pays 2 to 1. A bet on red or black, odd or even, and 1 through 18 or 19 through 36 pays off at even money, 1 to 1. If you think you can bet on red *and* black, or odd *and* even, in order to play roulette and drink for free all night, think again. The green 0 or 00, which fall outside these two basic categories, will come up on average once every 19 spins of the wheel.

SLOT MACHINES

Around the turn of 20th century, Charlie Fey built the first slot in his San Francisco basement. Today hundreds of models accept everything from pennies to specially minted $500 tokens. The major advance in the game is the progressive jackpot. Banks of slots within a casino are connected by computer, and the jackpot total is displayed on a digital meter above the machines. Generally, the total increases by 5% of the wager. If you're playing a dollar machine, each time you pull the handle (or press the spin button), a nickel is added to the jackpot.

How to Play

To play, insert your penny, nickel, quarter, silver dollar, or dollar token into the slot at the far right edge of the machine. Pull the handle or press the spin button, and then wait for the reels to spin and stop one by one, and for the machine to determine whether you're a winner (occasionally) or a loser (the rest of the time). It's pretty simple, but because there are so many types of machines nowadays, be sure you know exactly how the one you're playing operates.

Slot-Machine Strategy

The house advantage on slots varies from machine to machine, between 3% and 25%. Casinos that advertise a 97% payback are telling you that at least one of their slot machines has a house advantage of 3%. Which one? There's really no way of knowing. Generally, $1 machines pay back at a higher percentage than quarter or nickel machines. On the other hand, machines with smaller jackpots pay back more money more frequently, meaning that you'll be playing with more of your winnings.

One of the all-time great myths about slot machines is that they're "due" for a jackpot. Slots, like roulette, craps, keno, and Big Six, are subject to the Law of Independent Trials, which means the odds are permanently and unalterably fixed. If the odds of lining up three sevens on a 25¢ slot machine have been set by the casino at 1 in 10,000, then those odds remain 1 in 10,000 whether the three 7s have been hit three times in a row or not hit for 90,000 plays. Don't waste a lot of time playing a machine that you suspect is "ready," and don't think if someone hits a jackpot on a particular machine only minutes after you've finished playing on it that it was "yours."

VIDEO POKER

This section deals only with straight-draw video poker.

Like blackjack, video poker is a game of strategy and skill, and at select times on select machines, the player actually holds the advantage, however slight, over the house. Unlike with slot machines, you can determine the exact edge of video-poker machines. Like slots, however, video-poker machines are often tied into a progressive meter; when the jackpot total reaches high enough, you can beat the casino at its own game. The variety of video-poker machines is growing steadily. All are played in similar fashion, but the strategies are different.

How to Play

The schedule for the payback on winning hands is posted on the machine, usually above the screen. It lists the returns for a high pair (generally jacks or better), two pair, three of a kind, a flush, full house, straight flush, four of a kind, and royal flush, depending on the number of coins played—usually 1, 2, 3, 4, or 5. Look for machines that pay with a single coin played: 1 coin for "jacks or better" (meaning a pair of jacks, queens, kings, or aces; any other pair is a stiff), 2 coins for two pairs, 3 for three of a kind, 6 for a flush, 9 for a full house, 50 for a straight flush, 100 for four of a kind, and 250 for a royal flush. This is known as a 9/6 machine—one that gives a nine-coin payback for a full house and a six-coin payback for a flush with one coin played. Other machines are known as 8/5 (eight for a full house, five for a flush), 7/5, and 6/5.

You want a 9/6 machine because it gives you the best odds: the return from a standard 9/6 straight-draw machine is 99.5%; you give up only half a percent to the house. An 8/5 machine returns 97.3%. On 6/5 machines, the figure drops to 95.1%, slightly less than roulette. Machines with varying paybacks are scattered throughout the casinos. In some you'll see an 8/5 machine right next to a 9/6, and someone will be blithely playing the 8/5 machine.

As with slot machines, it's optimum to play the maximum number of coins to qualify for the jackpot. You insert five coins into the slot and press the "deal" button. Five cards appear on the screen—say, 5, jack, queen, 5, 9. To hold the pair of 5s, you press the hold buttons under the first and fourth cards. The word "hold" appears underneath the two 5s. You then press the "draw" button (often the same button as "deal") and three new cards appear on the screen—say, 10, jack, 5. You have three 5s. With five coins bet, the machine will give you 15 credits. Now you can press the "max bet" button: five units will be removed from your credits, and five new cards will appear on the screen. You repeat the hold and draw process; if you hit a winning hand, the proper payback will be added to your credits. Those who want coins rather than credit can hit the "cash out" button at any time. Some machines don't have credit counters and automatically dispense coins for a winning hand.

Video-Poker Strategy

Like blackjack, video poker has a basic strategy that's been formulated by the computer simulation of hundreds of millions of hands. The most effective way to learn it is with a video poker–

computer program that deals the cards on your screen, then tutors you in how to play each hand properly. If you don't want to devote that much time to the study of video poker, memorizing these six rules will help you make the right decision for more than half the hands you'll be dealt:

If you're dealt a completely "stiff" hand (no like cards and no picture cards), draw five new cards.

If you're dealt a hand with no like cards but with one jack, queen, king, or ace, always hold on to the picture card; if you're dealt two different picture cards, hold both. But if you're dealt three different picture cards, hold only two (the two of the same suit, if that's an option).

If you're dealt a pair, hold it, no matter the face value.

Never hold a picture card with a pair of 2s through 10s.

Never draw two cards to try for a straight or a flush.

Never draw one card to try for an inside straight.

A guide leads a small group of hikers along a dusty path lined with watapana trees. Walking between the rock formations and giant cacti, the hikers laugh about the heat and chat about their plans for the rest of the day. "Quiet please!", the guide shouts. The group stops and heeds his request. They listen to the sounds of birds chirping and bending branches creaking in the constant breeze. "That is the sound of Aruba," the guide says—the hikers nod in silent understanding.

In This Chapter

outdoor activities & sports

ABOVE THE SURFACE AND BELOW, Aruban waters are brimming with activity. Although beach bumming is a popular pastime, golf, tennis, and horseback riding are also good options. More adventurous souls can explore the terrain on a motorcycle, parasail through the Aruban sky, or harness the power of the wind on a kiteboard. Constant trade winds have made Aruba an internationally recognized windsurfing destination. The crystalline waters of the island's leeward side offer scuba divers and snorkelers a kaleidoscopic adventure day or night.

You probably won't find Arubans singing "Take Me Out to the Ball Game," but come time for soccer season (late May–November, with matches on Tuesday, Thursday, Saturday, and Sunday) or track-and-field meets, and some 3,200 spirited people pack into the **COMPLEHO DEPORTIVO GUILLERMO PROSPERO TRINIDAD** (Stadionweg, Oranjestad, tel. 297/582–9550). Events at this complex open with the Aruban national anthem, a display of flags, and the introduction of any old-timers in the stadium. Adult admission ranges from $3 to $6, depending on whether it's a local or international competition; children get in for just over a dollar. Regardless of what's on, you won't find vendors hawking hot dogs or cotton candy. The snack bar sells such Aruban favorites as *pastechi* (meat-, cheese-, or seafood-filled turnovers) and *bitterballen* (bite-size meatballs), which you can wash down with a soda or a local Balashi beer.

Sidney Ponson: Pitcher

When he was growing up in Aruba, Sidney Ponson loved sailing, scuba diving, and just about anything to do with the ocean. "My life was the beach," says Ponson, "before baseball." He started playing baseball when he was 9, even though the game was pretty difficult on an arid island where the fields are full of rocks. But employment on his uncle's boat taught him to work hard for what he wanted in life.

The pitcher signed with the minor leagues at 16, then was tapped by the Baltimore Orioles by the time he was 21. Hitting the big leagues involved lots of hard work (his grueling workouts last from 7:30 AM to 1 PM and involve lifting weights, running, and throwing), but Ponson says it was worth it when he got the call to play. "It was 6:30 AM, and I was on a road trip in a hotel in Scranton," he remembers. "They told me when to show up and said to be ready to play at 8:30."

Now, Ponson spends 10 months a year in the United States pitching for his current team, the St. Louis Cardinals, and two months in Aruba resting and visiting family and friends. Ponson uses his status as a major leaguer to do some good for his island. He and fellow Aruban baseball player Calvin Maduro draft other professional baseball players, including Pedro Martinez and Manny Ramirez, to play in an annual celebrity softball game to raise funds for Aruba's Cas pa Hubentud, a home for underprivileged children.

To prepare for a game, Ponson heads to the clubhouse for some serious stretching to the hard-rock music of Metallica, AC/DC, or Mötley Crüe. How does it feel right before he heads out to pitch? "One million people want to do what I do—play ball in front of 50,000 people every night," says Ponson, "and that's a great feeling."

BEACHES

The beaches on Aruba are legendary: white sand, turquoise waters, and virtually no litter—everyone takes the NO TIRA SUSHI (NO LITTERING) signs very seriously, especially considering the island's $280 fine. The major public beaches, which back up to the hotels along the southwestern strip, are usually crowded. Make sure you're well protected from the sun—it scorches fast despite the cooling trade winds. Luckily, there's at least one covered bar (and often an ice-cream stand) at virtually every hotel. On the island's northeastern side, stronger winds make the waters too choppy for swimming, but the vistas are great and the terrain is wonderful for exploring.

ARASHI BEACH. The water is calm, the swimming is fine, and the white, powdery sands are shaded by some huts (though there are no other facilities). The beach is a 10-minute walk from the last bus stop on Malmok Beach and is accessible by car or taxi.

★ **BABY BEACH.** On the island's eastern tip, this semicircular beach borders a bay that's as placid and just about as shallow as a wading pool—perfect for tots, shore divers, and terrible swimmers. Thatched shaded areas are good for cooling off. Stop by the nearby snack truck for burgers, hot dogs, beer, and soda.

BOCA CATALINA. Although there are some stones and pebbles along this white-sand beach, snorkelers come for the shallow water filled with fish. Swimmers will also appreciate the calm conditions. There aren't any facilities nearby, however, so pack provisions.

BOCA GRANDI. Strong swimming skills are a must at this beach near the island's eastern tip.

BOCA PRINS. You'll need a four-wheel-drive vehicle to make the trek here. The beach is about as large as a Brazilian bikini, but people don't come here to swim. With two rocky cliffs and crashing waves, the scenery is incredibly romantic. Boca Prins is also famous for its backdrop of enormous vanilla-sand dunes. Bring a picnic, a beach blanket, and sturdy sneakers, and descend the rocks that form steps to the water's edge.

BOCA TABLA. This east-side beach, also called Bachelor's Beach, is known for its white-powder sand and good snorkeling and windsurfing. Don't head here for the swimming (conditions aren't the best) or the facilities (there aren't any).

DOS PLAYA. Hire a four-wheel-drive vehicle, pack a blanket and a picnic basket, and head here to take in the beautiful view. Swimming is discouraged because of strong currents and massive waves.

DRUIF. Fine white sand and calm water make this "tops-optional" beach a fine choice for sunbathing and swimming. Convenience is a highlight, too: hotels are close at hand, and the beach is accessible by bus, rental car, or taxi.

★ **EAGLE BEACH.** On the southwestern coast, across the highway from what is quickly becoming known as Time-Share Lane, is what is rightfully considered one of the best beaches in the world. Not long ago Eagle Beach was a nearly deserted stretch of pristine sand dotted with the occasional thatched picnic hut. Now that the resorts are completed, this mile-plus-long beach is always hopping.

FISHERMAN'S HUTS. This beach, also called Hadikurari, is a windsurfer's haven. In fact, it's the site for the annual Hi-Winds Pro-Am Windsurfing Competition. But any day you can take a picnic lunch (tables are available) and watch the elegant purple, aqua, and orange sails catching the breeze. The swimming conditions are good here as well, though the sand has some pebbles and stones.

GRAPEFIELD BEACH. To the northeast of San Nicolas, this sweep of blinding white sand in the shadow of cliffs and boulders is marked by a memorial shaped like an anchor, dedicated to all seamen. Pick sea grapes in high season (January–June). Swim at your own risk, as the waves here can be rough.

MALMOK BEACH. On the northwestern shore, this small, nondescript beach (where some of Aruba's wealthiest families have built residences) borders shallow waters that stretch 300 yards from shore. It's the perfect place to learn to windsurf. Right off the coast here is a favorite haunt for divers and snorkelers—the wreck of the German ship *Antilla*, scuttled in 1940.

MANGEL HALTO. Drive or cab it over to this east-side beach, also known as Savaneta. It's a lovely setting for a picnic. Hop into the shallow waters for a swim after taking in the sun on the fine white sand.

PALM BEACH. This stretch runs from the Wyndham Aruba Beach Resort & Casino to the Marriott's Aruba Ocean Club. It's the center of Aruban tourism, offering the best in swimming, sailing, and other water sports. In some spots you might find a variety of shells that are great to collect, but not as much fun to step on barefoot—bring sandals just in case.

PUNTA BRABO. In front of the Manchebo Beach Resort, this impressively wide stretch of white powder, also called Manchebo Beach, is where officials turn a blind eye to the occasional topless sunbather.

RODGER'S BEACH. Next to Baby Beach on the island's eastern tip, this beautiful curving stretch of sand is only slightly marred by the view of the oil refinery at the bay's far side. Swimming conditions are excellent here, as demonstrated by the local kids diving off the piers. The snack bar at the water's edge has beach-equipment rentals and a shop. Local bands play Sunday nights from Easter through summer.

SANTO LARGO. Swimming conditions are good—thanks to shallow water edged by white-powder sand—but there are no facilities at this beach west of Mangel Halto.

SURFSIDE. Accessible by public bus, car, or taxi, this beach is the perfect place to swim. It's also conveniently located next to the Havana Beach Club and across the street from the Caribbean Town Beach Resort.

ACTIVITIES

Adventure Games

Paintball aficionados can unite in a messier version of capture the flag. The game is played with air guns that propel biodegradable gelatin capsules that splatter you with water-soluble paint on impact. To win, simply return the opposing team's flag to your own team's station without being hit by a pellet. Games (complete with equipment and protective gear) are run by **EVENTS IN MOTION** (Rancho Daimari, Tanki Leendert 249, Plantage Daimari, tel. 297/587–5675, www.visitaruba.com/ranchodaimari). Games last about two hours, costing $40 per person with a minimum of 10 people. You must make reservations three days in advance.

Biking & Motorcycling

Pedal pushing is a great way to get around the island; the climate is perfect, and the trade winds help keep you cool. **PABLITO'S BIKE & LOCKER RENTAL** (L. G. Smith Blvd. 234, Oranjestad, tel. 297/587–8655) rents mountain bikes for $15 a day.

If you prefer to exert less energy while reaping the rewards of the outdoors, a scooter is a great way to whiz from place to place. Or let your hair down completely and cruise around on a Harley Davidson. **BIG TWIN ARUBA** (L. G. Smith Blvd. 124-A, Oranjestad, tel. 297/582–8660, www.harleydavidson-aruba.com) fulfills every biker's fantasy. With an initial $1,000 deposit, rates are $149 for a day or $99 for a half day (including insurance and helmets). The dealership also sells Harley clothing, accessories, and collectibles. Be sure to pose for a photo next to the classic 1939 Liberator on display in the showroom. The shop is open Monday through Saturday from 9 to 6.

There are plenty of dealers around who will be happy to help you in your motoring pursuits. **DONATA CAR AND CYCLE** (L. G. Smith Blvd. 136-D, Oranjestad, tel. 297/583–4343) rents motorcycles and mopeds. For scooters and all-terrain vehicles, head to **GEORGE'S CYCLE CENTER** (L. G. Smith Blvd. 136, Oranjestad, tel. 297/592–5875). **SEMVER CYCLE RENTAL** (Noord 22, Noord, tel. 297/586–6851) will help you choose the motorcycle or scooter that matches your experience level and your plans for the day.

If you prefer motoring with folks who are in the know, **DE PALM TOURS** (L. G. Smith Blvd. 142, Oranjestad, tel. 297/582–4400 or 800/766–6016, www.depalm.com) offers four- to eight-hour guided tours on all-terrain vehicles that pass through Arikok National Park en route to Natural Bridge. Prices range from $75 to $100. De Palm also conducts an all-day four-wheel-drive tour called the Aruba Safari, one of the most popular trips on the island. The cost is $59 to $75. These trips give you plenty of time to swim, and sometimes include lunch.

Bowling

The **EAGLE BOWLING PALACE** (Sasakiweg, Pos Abou, Oranjestad, tel. 297/583–5038) has 12 lanes, a snack bar, and a cocktail lounge. It opens Monday and Tuesday at 5 PM, the rest of the week at 10 AM, and doesn't close until 2 AM. Children under 12 can bowl until 7 PM. One lane for one hour will cost $10 to $12, depending on the time of day.

Fishing

Deep-sea catches here include barracuda, kingfish, blue and white marlin, wahoo, bonito, and black and yellow tuna. Each October, the island hosts the International White Marlin Competition. Many skippered charter boats are available for half- or full-day trips. Packages include tackle, bait, and refreshments. Prices range from $220 to $320 for a half-day charter and from $400 to $600 for a full day. Contact **DE PALM TOURS** (L. G. Smith Blvd. 142, Oranjestad, tel. 297/582–4400 or 800/766–6016, www.depalm.com) for a choice of fishing excursions. **PELICAN TOURS & WATERSPORTS** (Pelican Pier, near the Holiday Inn and Playa Linda hotels, Palm Beach, tel. 297/586–3271, www.pelican-aruba.com) is not just for the surf and snorkel crowd; the company will help you catch trophy-size fish. **RED SAIL SPORTS** (J. E. Irausquin Blvd. 83, Oranjestad, tel. 297/586–1603, 877/733–7245 in U.S., www.aruba-redsail.com) will arrange everything for your fishing trip. **TEASER CHARTERS** (St. Vincentweg 5, Oranjestad, tel. 297/582–5088, www.teasercharters.com) provides the hook and line, but the sinker is up to you.

Golf

Golf may seem incongruous on an arid island such as Aruba, yet there are several popular courses. The constant trade winds and occasional stray goat add unexpected hazards.

The **ARUBA GOLF CLUB** (Golfweg 82, San Nicolas, tel. 297/584–2006) has a 9-hole course with 20 sand traps and 5 water traps, roaming goats, and lots of cacti. There are also 11 greens covered with artificial turf, making 18-hole tournaments a possibility. The clubhouse has a bar and locker rooms. Greens fees are $10 for 9 holes, $15 for 18 holes. Golf carts are available.

ARUBA GOLF & LEISURE (J. E. Irasquin Blvd. 326, Oranjestad, tel. 297/586–4590) has a 300-yard driving range, an 18-hole putting green, and a chipping area. A bucket of balls will set you back $3, and you can rent a half set of clubs for $10. It's open from 7 AM to 11 PM daily.

A moat surrounds the pair of elevated 18-hole miniature golf courses at **ADVENTURE GOLF & FUN PARK** (Joe Mendez Miniature Adventure Golf, Sasakiweg, Oranjestad, tel. 297/588–6576). There are also paddleboats and bumper boats, a snack stand, and a bar. A round of 18 holes costs $7. It's open 5 PM to 1 AM during the week and from noon to 1 AM on the weekends.

Golfers can rejoice, because **THE LINKS AT DIVI ARUBA** (J. E. Irasquin Blvd. 93, Oranjestad, tel. 297/525–5200), a 9-hole golf course designed by Karl Litten and Lorie Viola, is the newest course on the island. The lush par-36 course on paspalum grass (best for seaside courses) takes you past beautiful lagoons. Amenities include a golf school with professional instruction, a swing analysis station, a driving range, and a two-story golf clubhouse with a pro shop. A tasty meal at one of the two restaurants, the upscale Windows on Aruba and the more casual Mulligan's Bistro, is par for the course.

★ On the northwest coast, **TIERRA DEL SOL GOLF COURSE** (Malmokweg, tel. 297/586–0978) is a stunner. Designed by Robert Trent Jones Jr., this 18-hole championship course combines Aruba's native beauty—cacti and rock formations—with the lush greens of the world's best courses. The three knockouts are Hole 3, perched on a cliff overlooking the sea; Hole 14, with a saltwater marsh inhabited by wild egrets; and Hole 16, whose fairway rolls along dunes. The $133 greens fee ($70 in summer) includes a golf cart equipped with a communications system that allows you to order drinks that will be ready upon your return. Half-day golf clinics, a bargain at $45, include lunch in the clubhouse. The pro shop is one of the Caribbean's most elegant, with an extremely attentive staff. Package vacations with villa rentals are available.

Hiking

There are more than 34 km (20 mi) of trails in **ARIKOK NATIONAL PARK** (tel. 297/582–8001), concentrated in the island's eastern interior and along its northeastern coast. The park is crowned by Aruba's second-highest mountain, the 577-foot Mt. Arikok, so climbing is also a possibility.

Hiking in the park, whether alone or in a group led by guides, is generally not too strenuous. Look for different colors to determine the degree of difficulty of each trail. Sturdy shoes are a must to grip the granular surfaces and climb the occasionally steep terrain. You should also exercise caution with the strong sun—bring along plenty of water and wear sunscreen and a hat.

The Aruban government is working on a 10-year ecotourism plan to preserve the resources of the park, which makes up 18% of the island's total area. The effort includes setting aside areas for recreation, establishing zones where the natural habitats are protected, and developing a scenic loop roadway. At the park's main entrance, the Arikok Center houses offices, restrooms, and food facilities. Under the plan, all visitors stop here upon entering so that officials can manage the traffic flow and distribute information on park rules and features.

Horseback Riding

Several ranches offer short jaunts along the beach or longer rides along trails passing through countryside flanked by cacti, divi-divi trees, and aloe-vera plants. Ask if you can stop off at Cura di Tortuga, a natural pool that's reputed to have restorative powers. Rides are also possible in the Arikok National Park. Rates run from $25 for an hourlong trip to $65 for a three-hour tour. Private rides cost slightly more.

DE PALM TOURS (L. G. Smith Blvd. 142, Oranjestad, tel. 297/582–4400 or 800/766–6016, www.depalm.com) arranges horseback-

Wildlife Watching

Wildlife abounds on Aruba. Look for the cottontail rabbit: the black patch on its neck likens it to a species found in Venezuela, spawning a theory that it was brought to the island by pre-Columbian peoples. Wild donkeys, originally transported to the island by the Spanish, are found in the more rugged terrain; sheep and goats roam freely throughout the island.

About 170 bird species make their home on Aruba year-round, and migratory birds temporarily raise the total to 300 species when they fly by in November and January. Among the highlights are the trupiaal (which is bright orange), the prikichi (a parakeet with a green body and yellow head), and the barika geel (a small, yellow-bellied bird with a sweet tooth—you may find one eating the sugar off your breakfast table). At Bubali Bird Sanctuary on the island's western side, you can see various types of waterfowl, especially cormorants, herons, scarlet ibis, and fish eagles. Along the south shore, brown pelicans are common. At Tierra del Sol Golf Course in the north, you may glimpse the shoko, the endangered burrowing owl.

Lizard varieties include large iguanas, once hunted for use in local soups and stews. (That practice is now illegal.) Like chameleons, these iguanas change color to adapt to their surroundings—from bright green when foraging in the foliage (which they love to eat) to a brownish shade when sunning themselves in the dirt. The pega pega—a cousin of the gecko—is named for the suction pads on its feet that allow it to grip virtually any surface (pega means "to stick" in Papiamento). The kododo blauw (whiptail lizard) is one of the species that is unique to the island.

Two types of snakes are found only on Aruba. The cat-eyed santanero isn't venomous, but it won't hesitate to defecate in your hand should you pick it up. The poisonous cascabel is a unique subspecies of rattlesnake that doesn't use its rattle. These snakes live in the area between Mt. Yamanota, Fontein, and San Nicolas.

riding excursions. **RANCHO DEL CAMPO** (Sombre 22E, Santa Cruz, tel. 297/585–0290, www.ranchodelcampo.com), the first to offer rides to Natural Pool back in 1991, leads various excursions that start at $60 per person. **RANCHO DAIMARI** (Tanki Leendert 249 San Nicholas, tel. 297/587–5674, www.visitaruba.com/ranchodaimari) will lead your horse to water—in this case, Natural Pool—in the morning or afternoon for $60 per person. The "Junior Dudes" program is tailored for young riders. **RANCHO NOTORIOUS** (Boroncana, Noord, tel. 297/586–0508, www.ranchonotorious.com) will take you on a tour of the countryside or to the beach to snorkel for $65, or on a three-hour ride up to the California Lighthouse for $75.

Jet Skiing

If zipping through aqua-blue water at unholy speeds is your idea of fun, then renting a jet ski may be the way to go. Rentals are available in the water-sports centers at most hotels. Average prices for a half-hour ride are $45 for a single jet ski and $55 for a double. There are a few operators on the island, two of which are well regarded. **PELICAN TOURS & WATERSPORTS** (Pelican Pier, near the Holiday Inn and Playa Linda hotels, Palm Beach, tel. 297/586–3271, www.pelican-aruba.com) offers jet skis and wave runners. **UNIQUE SPORTS OF ARUBA** (L. G. Smith Blvd. 79, Oranjestad, tel./fax 297/586–0096 or 297/586–3900, www.visitaruba.com/uniquesports), operating exclusively from the Aruba Grand Beach Resort on Palm Beach, rents single and double jet skis.

Kayaking

Kayaking is a popular sport on Aruba, especially because the waters are so calm. It's a great way to explore the coast. Every day except Sunday, **DE PALM TOURS** (L. G. Smith Blvd. 142, Oranjestad, tel. 297/582–4400 or 800/766–6016, www.depalm.com) offers a four-hour guided kayaking tour that includes some snorkeling. The cost, including lunch, is $80.

Kiteboarding

Thanks to constant trade winds, kiteboarding (also called kitesurfing) is fast becoming a popular pastime on this tiny island. The sport involves gliding on and above the water on a small surfboard or wakeboard while hooked up to an inflatable kite. Windsurfing experience helps, and practice time on the beach is essential. Those eager to fly the friendly skies can take lessons and ★ rent reliable equipment at Vela Windsurf's **FISHERMAN'S HUTS WINDSURF CENTER** (L. G. Smith Blvd. 101, Palm Beach, tel. 297/586–9000 Ext. 6430 or 800/223–5443, www.velawindsurf.com). Another kiteboarding operator is **ARUBA BOARDSAILING PRODUCTIONS** (L. G. Smith Blvd. 486, Palm Beach, tel. 297/586–3940 or 297/993–1111, www.visitaruba.com/arubaboardsailing). Kiteboarding rental costs are usually a reasonable $55 per day (though it may take the better part of a day to get the hang of it). Once you're proficient, you may want to pursue some of the island's freestyle tournaments and long-distance races.

Parasailing

For about 12 exhilarating minutes, motorboats at Palm and Eagle beaches tow you up and over the waters around Aruba ($55 for a single-seater, $80 for a tandem). You can make arrangements with your hotel, or through independent operators stationed on the beaches. **CARIBBEAN PARASAIL** (tel. 297/586–0505) is one of the island's top operators. Working with many hotels, **PELICAN TOURS & WATERSPORTS** (Pelican Pier, near the Holiday Inn and the Playa Linda hotels, Palm Beach, tel. 297/586–3271, www.pelican-aruba.com) has equipment for parasailing and other outdoor activities. Although it's best known for its diving trips, **RED SAIL SPORTS** (J. E. Irausquin Blvd. 83, tel. 297/586–1603, 877/733–7245 in U.S., www.aruba-redsail.com) will also take you parasailing.

Playgrounds

You can let the kids run loose in **KIBAIMA MINIATURE VILLAGE** (Kibaima 5, south of the airport across Hwy. 4 from the outdoor theater, Oranjestad, tel. 297/585–1830 or 297/585–1980), a little park filled with scaled-down versions of typical Aruban houses. There are also plenty of exotic birds and animals. The park is open daily from 10 AM to 6 PM, with daily 10 AM tours. The $5 admission charge for children under 12 years old and $10 fee for adults includes a tour. **TIRA KOOCHI PARK** (Savaneta 338A, Oranjestad) is open daily from 4 PM to 6:30 PM daily. The playground is behind Prome Paso School.

Sailing

You can have a hull of a good time sailing around Aruba on a Sunfish, or you can opt for a daytime or sunset sail aboard a trimaran or catamaran. The **SEAPORT MARINA** (Seaport Marketplace 204, Oranjestad) is the place to go for charters.

DE PALM TOURS (L. G. Smith Blvd. 142, Oranjestad, tel. 297/582–4400 or 800/766–6016, www.depalm.com) will sail you over the open seas for a two- to four-hour snorkeling adventure at nearby reefs. The cost for the catamaran trip is $37 to $59 per person. **MI DUSHI** (Turibana Plaza, Noord 124, Noord, tel. 297/586–2010, www.midushi.com), a ship whose name means "My Sweetheart," will sail you into the sunset with yours for $25 per person. Daytime snorkeling trips on this romantic two-masted ship include breakfast, lunch, and drinks for $59 per person. **PELICAN TOURS & WATERSPORTS** (Pelican Pier, near the Holiday Inn and Playa Linda hotels, Palm Beach, tel. 297/586–3271, www.pelican-aruba.com) offers daytime snorkeling trips to two different reefs for about $35 per person. The company also offers sunset sails for the same price that can be combined with dinner at the Pelican Restaurant on Palm Beach. **RED SAIL SPORTS** (J. E. Irausquin Blvd. 83, Oranjestad, tel. 297/586–1603, 877/733–7245 in U.S., www.aruba-redsail.com) serves you lunch and lets you snorkel at two different sites for $59 per person. There's also a sunset cruise for $37.50 per person.

Scuba Diving & Snorkeling

With visibility of up to 90 feet, the waters around Aruba are excellent for snorkeling and diving. Both advanced and novice divers will find plenty to occupy their time, as many of the most popular sites, including some interesting shipwrecks, are found in shallow waters ranging from 30 feet to 60 feet. Coral reefs covered with sensuously waving sea fans and eerie giant sponge tubes attract a colorful menagerie of sea life, including gliding manta rays, curious sea turtles, shy octopuses, and fish from grunts to groupers. Note that marine preservation is a priority on Aruba, and regulations by the Conference on International Trade in Endangered Species make it unlawful to remove coral, conch, and other marine life from the water.

Most resorts offer diving courses for beginners that include instruction and all equipment; those seeking advanced certification can do so through any of the island's licensed dive centers. Some popular dive sites are listed below, but be sure to pick up the Aruba Tourism Authority's brochure, "The Island for Water Sports," which describes many more.

OPERATORS

Expect snorkel gear to rent for about $15 per day and snorkeling trips to cost around $40. Scuba rates are around $35 for a one-tank reef or wreck dive, $60 for a two-tank dive, and $40 for a night dive. Resort courses, which offer an introduction to scuba diving, average $75. If you want to go all the way, complete open-water certification costs around $350. Many operators will pick you up and drop you off at your hotel at no additional cost.

The more seasoned diving crowd might check with **ARUBA PRO DIVE** (Ponton 88, Noord, tel. 297/582–5520, www.arubaprodive.com) for special deals. **DAX DIVERS** (Kibaima 7, Santa Cruz, tel.

297/585–1270) has an instructor training course. Some dives are less expensive, at $40 for 40 minutes with one tank and weights.
★ **DE PALM TOURS** (L. G. Smith Blvd. 142, Oranjestad, tel. 297/582–4400 or 800/766–6016, www.depalm.com) is one of the best options for your undersea experience, and the options go beyond basic diving. Don a helmet and walk along the ocean floor near De Palm Island, home of huge blue parrot fish. Have your picture taken at an underwater table loaded with champagne glasses and roses. Try Snuba—like scuba diving but without the heavy air tanks—either from a boat or from an island. It's $55 when you book another activity. **DIVE ARUBA** (Williamstraat 8, Oranjestad, tel. 297/582–4554, www.divearuba.com) offers resort courses, certification courses, and trips to interesting shipwrecks. At Manchebo Beach Resort, **MERMAID SPORT DIVERS** (J. E. Irausquin Blvd. 55A, Eagle Beach, tel. 297/587–4103, www.scubadivers-aruba.com) has dive packages with PADI-certified instructors.

NATIVE DIVERS ARUBA (Koyari 1, Noord, tel. 297/586–4763, www.nativedivers.com) offers all types of dives. Courses in specialties such as underwater naturalist are taught by PADI-certified instructors. **PELICAN TOURS & WATERSPORTS** (Pelican Pier, near the Holiday Inn and Playa Linda hotels, Palm Beach, tel. 297/586–3271, www.pelican-aruba.com) has options for divers of all levels. Novices start with midmorning classes and then move to the pool to practice what they've learned; by afternoon they put their new skills to use at a shipwreck off the coast. **RED SAIL SPORTS** (J. E. Irausquin Blvd. 83, Oranjestad, tel. 297/586–1603, 877/733–7245 in U.S., www.aruba-redsail.com) has courses for children and others new to scuba diving. An introductory class costs about $80.

SEARUBA FLY 'N DIVE (Shiribana 9A, Paradera, tel. 297/587–8759, www.searuba.com) will take you higher and lower than you ever thought possible in one day. You can take aerial shots from above the dive sites, then dive underwater. They even offer a two-day diving adventure in Bonaire (the reefs are much better there) that includes flight, accommodations, and diving for

$340. Aside from the usual diving courses, the company can also instruct your group in rescue techniques. At the Aruba Grand Beach Resort, **UNIQUE SPORTS OF ARUBA** (L. G. Smith Blvd. 79, Oranjestad, tel. 297/586–0096 or 297/586–3900, www.visitaruba.com/uniquesports) lives up to its name, providing dive master, rescue, and certification courses.

WEST-SIDE DIVE SITES

ANTILLA WRECK. This German freighter, which sank off the northwest coast near Malmok Beach, is very popular with both divers and snorkelers. Scuttled during World War II not long after its maiden voyage, the 400-foot-long vessel—referred to by locals as "the ghost ship"—has large compartments. You can climb into the captain's bathtub, which sits beside the wreck, for a unique photo op. Lobster, angelfish, yellowtail, and other fish swim about the wreck, which is blanketed by giant tube sponges and coral.

BARCADERA REEF. Only large types of coral—staghorn, elkhorn, pillar—find their niche close to this reef because the sand makes it difficult for the smaller varieties to survive. The huge (and abundant) sea fans here wave in the current.

BLACK BEACH. The clear waters just off this beach are dotted with sea fans. The area takes its name from the rounded black stones lining the shore. It's the only bay on the island's north coast sheltered from thunderous waves, making it a safe spot for diving.

CALIFORNIAN WRECK. Although this steamer is submerged at a depth that's perfect for underwater photography, this site is safe only for advanced divers; the currents here are strong, and the waters are dangerously choppy.

HARBOUR REEF. Steeply sloped boulders surrounded by a multitude of soft coral formations make this a great spot for novices. The calm waters are noteworthy for their abundance of fascinating plant life.

MALMOK REEF. Lobsters and stingrays are among the highlights at this bottom reef adorned by giant green, orange, and purple barrel sponges as well as leaf and brain coral. From here you can spot the *Debbie II*, a 120-foot barge that sank in 1992.

PEDERNALES WRECK. During World War II, this oil tanker was torpedoed by a German submarine. The U.S. military cut out the damaged centerpiece, towed the two remaining pieces to the States, and welded them together into a smaller vessel that eventually transported troops during the invasion of Normandy. The section that was left behind in shallow water is now surrounded by coral formations, making this a good site for novice divers. The ship's cabins, washbasins, and pipelines are exposed. The area teems with grouper and angelfish.

SKELETON CAVE. Human bones found here (historians hypothesize that they're remains of ancient Arawak people) gave this dive spot its name. A large piece of broken rock forms the entrance where the cave meets the coast.

SONESTA REEF. Two downed planes are the centerpiece of this interesting dive site near Sonesta Island. Several types of brain coral abound in this sandy-bottom area.

TUGBOAT WRECK. Spotted eagle rays and stingrays are sometimes observed at this shipwreck at the foot of Harbour Reef, making it one of Aruba's most popular. Spectacular formations of brain, sheet, and star coral blanket the path to the wreck, which is inhabited by a pair of bright green moray eels.

EAST-SIDE DIVE SITES

CAPTAIN ROGER WRECK. A plethora of colorful fish swish about this old tugboat, which rests off the coast at Seroe Colorado. From shore you can swim to a steep coral reef.

ISLA DI ORO. A wide expanse of reef grows far out along the shallow bank, making for superb diving. You'll be treated to views of green moray eels, coral crabs, trumpet fish, and French, gray, and queen angelfish.

JANE WRECK. This 200-foot freighter, lodged in an almost vertical position at a depth of 90 feet, is near the coral reef west of Palm Island. Night diving is exciting here, as the polyps emerge from the corals that grow profusely on the steel plates of the decks and cabins. Soft corals and sea fans are also abundant in the area.

PALM ISLAND. Secluded behind clusters of mangrove, the reef system around Palm Island stretches all the way to Oranjestad. You can get close enough to touch the nurse sharks that sleep tucked into reef crevices during the day.

PUNTA BASORA. This narrow reef stretches far into the sea off the island's easternmost point. On calm days you'll see eagle rays, stingrays, barracudas, and hammerhead sharks, as well as hawksbill and loggerhead turtles.

SHARK CAVES. At this site along the island's southeastern point you can swim alongside sand sharks and float past the nurse sharks sleeping under the rock outcroppings.

VERA WRECK. In 1954, this freighter sank while en route to North America. The crew, saved by an Aruban captain, claimed the ship held Nazi treasures.

THE WALL. From May to August, green sea turtles intent on laying their eggs abound at this steep-walled reef. You'll also spot long-branched gorgons, groupers, and burrfish swimming nearby. Close to shore, massive sheet corals are plentiful; in the upper part of the reef are colorful varieties such as black coral, star coral, and flower coral. Flitting about are brilliant damselfish, rock beauties, and porgies.

Tennis

Aruba's winds make tennis a challenge even if you have the best of backhands. Although visitors can make arrangements to play at the resorts, priority goes to guests. Some private tennis clubs can also accommodate you. Try the facilities at the **ARUBA RACQUET CLUB** (Rooisanto 21, Palm Beach, tel. 297/586–0215, www.arc.aw). Host to a variety of international tournaments, the club has eight courts (six lighted), as well as a swimming pool, an aerobics center, and a restaurant. Fees are $10 per hour; a lesson with a pro costs $20 for a half hour, $40 for one hour.

Windsurfing

Whisk through the waves and revel in the sea spray. Aruba has all it takes for windsurfing: trade winds that average 15 knots year-round (peaking May–July), a sunny climate, and perfect azure-blue waters. With a few lessons from a certified instructor, even novices will be jibing in no time. The southwestern coast's tranquil waters make it ideal for both beginners and intermediates, as the winds are steady but sudden gusts rare. Experts will find the waters of the Atlantic, especially around Grapefield and Boca Grandi beaches, more challenging; winds are fierce and often shift without warning. Rentals average about $60 a day, and lessons range from $50 to $125. Many hotels include windsurfing in their water-sports packages, and most operators can help you arrange complete windsurfing vacations.

Every June sees the Hi-Winds Pro-Am Windsurfing Competition, attracting professionals and amateurs from around the world. There are divisions for women, men, juniors, masters, and grand masters. Disciplines include slalom, course racing, long distance, and freestyle. The entry fee is $150, but there's a $25 discount if you register online at www.aruba-hiwinds.com.

ARUBA BEACH VILLAS (L. G. Smith Blvd. 462, Malmok Beach, tel. 297/586–2527, 800/320–9998 in U.S., www.sailboardvacations.com) offers first-rate instruction. It's at Windsurf Village, a lodging complex created by and for windsurfers near Fisherman's Huts, a world-renowned sailing spot. Another lure for those in the know: the complex is home to one of the Caribbean's largest and best-stocked windsurfing shops.

Trade jokes and snap photos with your fellow windsurfers at Vela Windsurf's **FISHERMAN'S HUTS WINDSURF CENTER** (L. G. Smith Blvd. 101, Palm Beach, tel. 297/586–9000 Ext. 6430 or 800/223–5443, www.velawindsurf.com/aruba), at the north end of the Marriott Hotel property in front of the Fisherman's Huts. This is *the* place to make friends on the water. **PELICAN TOURS & WATERSPORTS** (Pelican Pier, near the Holiday Inn and Playa Linda hotels, Palm Beach, tel. 297/586–3271, www.pelican-aruba.com) usually has boards and sails on hand. The day will fly by when you windsurf with **SAILBOARD VACATIONS** (L. G. Smith Blvd. 462, Malmok Beach, tel. 297/586–2527, www.sailboardvacations.com).

The guide points toward the rubble and, with more than a tinge of sadness, says "that used to be the Natural Bridge." The tourists look at pile of fallen stone in disappointment. "I suppose we could rebuild it," the guide muses. One member of the group chimes in, "but then it wouldn't be a natural bridge." "Oh, you just want to see a natural bridge?" the guide asks, "we have two more not too far from here. Let's go and see them." The group eagerly climbs back into the tour bus, which heads west in a cloud of dust. That's another one of Aruba's secrets—there's always something else to see.

In This Chapter

here & there

ARUBA'S WILDLY SCULPTED LANDSCAPE is replete with rocky deserts, cactus clusters, secluded coves, blue vistas, and the trademark divi-divi tree. To preserve the environment while encouraging visitors to explore, the government has implemented a 10-year, $10 million ecotourism plan. Initiatives include finding ways to make efficient use of the limited land resources and protecting the natural and cultural resources in such preserves as Arikok National Park and the Coastal Protection Zone (along the island's north and east coasts).

Oranjestad, Aruba's capital, is good for shopping by day and dining by night, but the "real Aruba"—with its untamed beauty—can be found only in the countryside. Rent a car, take a sightseeing tour, or hire a cab for $30 an hour. Though desolate, the northern and eastern shores are striking and well worth a visit. A drive out past the California Lighthouse or to Seroe Colorado will give you a feel for the backcountry.

Although the main highways are well paved, the windward side of the island still has some roads that are a mixture of compacted dirt and stones. A car is fine, but a four-wheel-drive vehicle will enable you to better navigate the unpaved interior. Remember that few beaches outside the hotel strip along Palm and Eagle beaches to the west have refreshment stands, so pack your own food and drink. Aside from those in the infrequent restaurant, there are no public bathrooms outside of Oranjestad.

Traffic is sparse, but signs leading to sights are often small and hand lettered (this is slowly changing as the government puts up

official road signs), so watch closely. Route 1A travels southbound along the western coast, and 1B is simply northbound along the same road. If you lose your way, just follow the divi-divi trees.

Numbers in the margin correspond to points of interest on the Exploring map.

WESTERN ARUBA

Western Aruba is where you'll likely spend most of your time. All the resorts and time-shares are along this coast, most of them clustered on the oceanfront strip at the luscious Palm and Eagle beaches, in the city of Oranjestad, or in the district of Noord. All the casinos, major shopping malls, and most restaurants are found in this region, as is the airport.

A Good Tour

Rent a car and head out on Route 1A toward **ORANJESTAD** ① for some sightseeing and shopping. Pick up Route 1B out of town. At a large roundabout turn right and drive for about 1 km (½ mi), then make another right at the first intersection and drive for ½ km (¼ mi) until you reach the fields and factory of **ARUBA ALOE** ②. Head back to the roundabout and pick up Route 4A. Follow this road a short way to the **AYO AND CASIBARI ROCK FORMATIONS** ③. Continue on 4A and follow the signs for **HOOIBERG** ④; if you're so inclined, climb the steps of Haystack Hill. Return on 4B to 6A and drive a couple of miles to the Bushiribana Gold Smelter. Beyond it on the windward coast is the **ARUBA OSTRICH FARM** ⑤.

From here, take 6B to the intersection of Route 3B, which you'll follow into the town of **NOORD** ⑥, a good place to stop for lunch. Then take Route 2B, following the signs for the branch road leading to the **ALTO VISTA CHAPEL** ⑦. Return to town and pick up 2B and then 1B to reach the **CALIFORNIA LIGHTHOUSE** ⑧. In this area you'll also see Arashi Beach (a popular snorkeling site) and the Tierra del Sol golf course. From the lighthouse follow 1A back toward Palm Beach. On the way, stop at the **BUTTERFLY FARM** ⑨ and the **BUBALI BIRD SANCTUARY** ⑩.

TIMING

If you head out right after breakfast, you can just about complete the tour above in one very full day. If you want to linger in Oranjestad's shops or go snorkeling along the beach, consider breaking the tour up into two days.

What to See

❼ **ALTO VISTA CHAPEL.** On the island's northwest corner, amid eerie boulders and looming cacti, sits the little Alto Vista Chapel. The wind whistles through the simple mustard-color walls. Along the side of the road back to civilization are miniature crosses depicting the stations of the cross and hand-lettered signs exhorting PRAY FOR US SINNERS and the like—a simple yet powerful evocation of faith. The chapel dates back to 1750 and has been completely restored. To get here, follow the rough, winding dirt road that loops around the island's northern tip. From the hotel strip, take Palm Beach Road through three intersections and watch for the asphalt road to the left just past the Alto Vista Rum Shop.

★ ❷ **ARUBA ALOE.** Learn all about this fascinating substance—its cultivation, processing, and production—at Aruba's own aloe farm and factory. Guided tours lasting about half an hour will show you how the gel—revered for its skin-soothing properties—is extracted from the aloe-vera plant and used in a variety of products, including after-sun creams, soaps, and shampoos. The tour may not quicken your pulse, but it is certainly useful for killing an hour on a rainy day. You can purchase the finished goods in the gift shop. *Pitastraat 115, Oranjestad, tel. 297/588–3222. www.arubaaloe.com. $6. Weekdays 8:30–4:30, Sat. 9–2.*

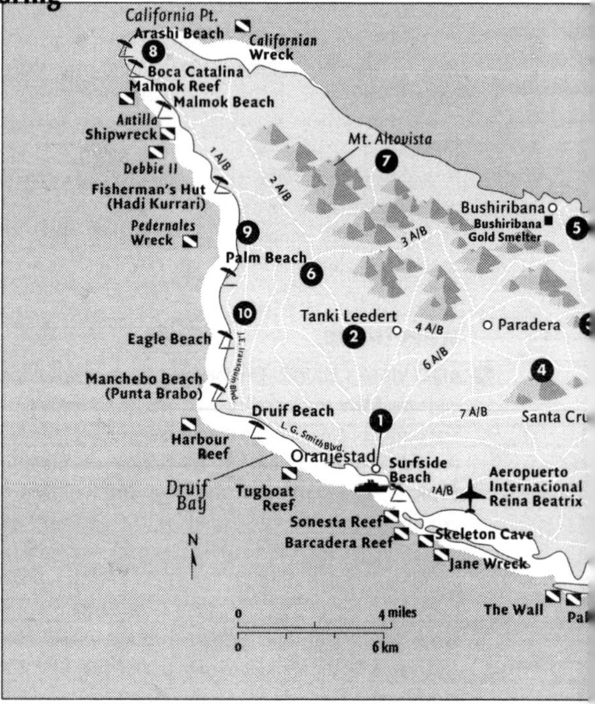

Alto Vista Chapel, **7**

Arikok National Park, **15**

Aruba Aloe, **2**

Aruba Ostrich Farm, **5**

Ayo and Casibari Rock Formations, **3**

Bubali Bird Sanctuary, **10**

Butterfly Farm, **9**

California Lighthouse, **8**

Frenchman's Pass, **11**

Hooiberg, **4**

Noord, **6**

Oranjestad, **1**

San Nicolas, **13**

Savaneta, **12**

Seroe Colorado, **14**

KEY
beaches
cruise-ship terminal
dive sites
Black Beach
Andicouri
Dos Playa
Boca Prins
15
Mt. Arikok
Fontein Cave
7 A/B
4 A/B
Miralamar
Guadirikiri Cave
Bananca Sunu
7B
7A
11
Masiduri Cave
Balashi Gold Mill Ruins
Spanish Lagoon
Mt. Yamanota
Boca Grandi
Balashi Brewery
Boca Table (Bachelor's Beach)
Mangel Halto (Savaneta)
13
1A
Natural Bridge
12
1 A/B
Captain Roger Wreck
n Reef
Mangel Halto Reef (Pos Chiquito Reef)
14
Santo Largo Beach
Grapefield Beach
Shark Caves
Isla di Oro
Rodger's Beach
Vera Wreck
Punta Basora
Baby Beach

★ 5 **ARUBA OSTRICH FARM.** Everything you've ever wanted to know about the world's largest living birds can be found at this farm. A large palapa houses a gift shop and restaurant (popular with bus tours), and tours are available every half-hour. After you are through admiring the noble beasts, you can chow down on them at the restaurant. The farm is virtually identical to the facility in Curaçao and is owned by the same company.

3 **AYO AND CASIBARI ROCK FORMATIONS.** The massive boulders at Ayo and Casibari are a mystery, as they don't match the island's geological makeup. You can climb to the top for fine views of the arid countryside. On the way you'll likely pass Aruba whiptail lizards—the males are cobalt blue, the females blue with dots. The main path to Casibari has steps and handrails (except on one side), and you must move through tunnels and along narrow steps and ledges to reach the top. At Ayo you'll find ancient pictographs in a small cave (the entrance has iron bars to protect the drawings from vandalism). You may also encounter boulder climbers, who are increasingly drawn to Ayo's smooth surfaces. Access to Casibari is via Tanki Highway 4A to Ayo via Route 6A; watch carefully for the turnoff signs near the center of the island on the way to the windward side.

10 **BUBALI BIRD SANCTUARY.** Bird-watchers delight in the more than 80 species of migratory birds that nest in this wetlands area inland from the island's strip of high-rise hotels. Herons, egrets, cormorants, coots, gulls, skimmers, terns, and ducks are among the winged wonders in and around the two interconnected artificial lakes that compose the sanctuary. *J. E. Irausquin Blvd., Noord, No phone. Free.*

★ 9 **BUTTERFLY FARM.** Hundreds of butterflies from around the world flutter by at this spectacular garden. Guided 20- to 30-minute tours (included in the price of admission) provide an entertaining look into how these creatures complete their life cycle: from egg to caterpillar to chrysalis to butterfly. Pay once and you can visit as many times as you like for the duration of your trip. *J. E. Irausquin*

Blvd., Palm Beach, tel. 297/586–3656. www.thebutterflyfarm.com. $12. Daily 9–4:30 (last tour at 4).

8 **CALIFORNIA LIGHTHOUSE.** This lighthouse, built by a French architect in 1910, stands at the island's far northern end. Although the interior is closed to the public, you can ascend the hill to its base for some great views. In this stark landscape, you'll feel as though you've just landed on the moon. The structure is surrounded by huge boulders that look like extraterrestrial monsters and sand dunes embroidered with scrub that resembles undulating sea serpents. Next to the nearby Trattoria El Farro Blanco—a great place to watch the sun set—there's a placard explaining the lighthouse's history and telling of the wreck of a German ship just offshore.

4 **HOOIBERG.** Named for its unusual shape (*hooiberg* means "haystack" in Dutch), this 541-foot peak lies inland just past the airport. Climb the 562 steps to the top for an impressive view of the city of Oranjestad. On a clear day, you can even see the northern coast of Venezuela.

6 **NOORD.** The district of Noord is home to the strip of high-rise hotels and casinos that line Palm Beach. Here you'll also find the beautiful St. Ann's Church, known for its ornate 19th-century altar. In this area, Aruban-style homes are scattered amid clusters of cacti.

1 **ORANJESTAD.** Aruba's charming capital is best explored on foot. Its palm-lined central thoroughfare runs between old and new pastel-painted buildings of typical Dutch design (Spanish influence is also evident in some of the architecture). There are many malls with boutiques and shops; downtown and Seaport Village are the major shopping areas. Every morning, the wharf teems with activity as merchants sell produce and fresh fish—often right off their boats. You can also buy handicrafts and T-shirts at this dockside bazaar, where bargaining is expected and dollars or florins are accepted. Island schooners and houseboats anchored

The Divi-Divi Tree

Like a statuesque dancer in a graceful flat-back pose, the watapana, or divi-divi tree, is one of Aruba's hallmarks. Oddly enough, this tropical shrub is a member of the legume family. Its astringent pods contain high levels of tannin, which is leached out for tanning leather. The pods also yield a black dye. The tree has a moderate rate of growth and a high drought tolerance. Typically it reaches no more than 25 feet in height, with a flattened crown and irregular, forked branches. Its leaves are dull green, and its inconspicuous yet fragrant flowers are pale yellow or white and grow in small clusters. Thanks to constant trade winds, the divi-divis serve as a natural compass: they're bent toward the island's leeward—or western—side, where most of the hotels are.

near the fishing boats add to the port's ambience. Wilhelmina Park, a small tropical garden on the waterfront along L. G. Smith Boulevard, has a sculpture of the Netherlands' Queen Wilhelmina, whose reign lasted from 1890 to 1948.

At the **Archaeological Museum of Aruba** you'll find two rooms chock-full of fascinating artifacts from Aruba's indigenous people, including farm and domestic utensils dating back hundreds of years. The skeletal remains on display are fascinating, and there are several books on the archaeological history of the island available for sale at the front desk. *J. E. Irausquinplein 2A, tel. 297/582–8979. Free. Weekdays 8–noon and 1–4.*

One of the island's oldest edifices, **Fort Zoutman** was built in 1796 and played an important role in skirmishes between British and Curaçao troops in 1803. The Willem III Tower, named for the

Dutch monarch of that time, was added in 1868 to serve as a lighthouse. Over time, the fort has been used as a government office building, a police station, and a prison. Now its historical museum displays Aruban artifacts in an 18th-century house. *Zoutmanstraat, tel. 297/582–6099. Free. Weekdays 8–noon and 1–4.*

★ The **Numismatic Museum** displays more than 40,000 historic coins and paper money from around the world. A few pieces were salvaged from shipwrecks in the region. Some of the coins circulated during the Roman Empire, the Byzantine Empire, and the ancient Chinese dynasties; the oldest dates to the 3rd century BC. The museum—which moved in 2003 to a new, larger location next to the central bus station—had its start as the private collection of one Aruban who dug up some old coins in his garden. It is now run by his granddaughter. *Westraat, tel. 297/582–8831. Free. Mon.–Thurs. 9–4, Fri. 9–1, Sat. 9–noon.*

The **Experience Aruba Panorama** brings the island's history and culture to life in a 22-minute cinematic extravaganza that fills five massive screens measuring 13 feet high and 66 feet wide. The breathtaking shows begin in the Crystal Theater at the Renaissance Aruba Beach Resort every hour from 11 to 5. *L. G. Smith Blvd. 82, tel. 297/583–6000. $10. Mon.–Sat. 11–5.*

Built in 1962, **Beth Israel Synagogue** is the only Jewish house of worship on Aruba, and it strives to meet the needs of its Ashkenazi, Sephardic, European, North American, and South American worshippers. The island's Jewish community dates back to the opening of the oil refinery in the 1920s, when small congregations gathered in private homes in San Nicolas. The temple holds regular services on Friday at 8 PM and on Saturday at 8 AM; additional services are held on High Holy Days. Visitors are always welcome, although it's best to make an appointment to see the synagogue when there's not a service. A Judaica shop sells keepsakes, kosher dry goods, and kiddush wines. *Adrian Laclé Blvd. 2, tel. 297/582–3272. Free except high holy days.*

EASTERN ARUBA

In addition to the vast Arikok National Park, eastern Aruba is home to the island's second-largest city, San Nicolas, and several charming fishing villages and pristine beaches. Here you'll get a real sense of traditional island life.

A Good Tour

Take Route 1A to Route 4B and visit the Balashi Gold Smelter ruins and **FRENCHMAN'S PASS** ⑪. Return to 1A and continue your drive past Mangel Halto Beach to **SAVANETA** ⑫, a fishing village and one of several residential areas that has examples of typical Aruban homes. Follow 1A to **SAN NICOLAS** ⑬, where you can meander along the main promenade, pick up a few souvenirs, and grab a bite to eat. Heading out of town, continue on 1A until you hit a fork in the road; follow the signs toward **SEROE COLORADO** ⑭, with the nearby natural bridge and the Colorado Point Lighthouse. From here, follow the signs toward Rodgers Beach, just one of several area shores where you can kick back for a while. Nearby Baby Beach, with calm waters and beautiful white sand, is a favorite spot for snorkelers. To the north, on Route 7B, is Boca Grandi, a great windsurfing spot. Next is Grapefield Beach, a stretch of white sand that glistens against a backdrop of cliffs and boulder formations. Shortly beyond it, on 7B, you'll come into **ARIKOK NATIONAL PARK** ⑮, where you can explore caves and tunnels, play on sand dunes, and tackle Mt. Yamanota, Aruba's highest elevation. Farther along 7B is Santa Cruz, where a wooden cross stands atop a hill to mark the spot where Christianity was introduced to the islanders. The same highway will bring you all the way into Oranjestad.

TIMING

You can follow the tour and see many of the sights in half a day, though it's easy to fill a full day if you spend time relaxing on a sandy beach or exploring the trails in Arikok National Park.

What to See

15 **ARIKOK NATIONAL PARK.** Nearly 20% of Aruba has been designated part of this national park, the keystone of the government's long-term ecotourism plan. Most of it sprawls across the interior, stretching to the north and encompassing a long strip of the windward shoreline. Within the confines of the park, near the island's center, is Mt. Arikok, the heart of a natural preserve that showcases the island's flora and fauna, the ruins of a gold-mining operation at Miralmar, and the remnants of Dutch peasant settlements at Masiduri. The 620-foot Mt. Yamanota, Aruba's highest peak, is also in the park.

Anyone looking for geological exotica should head for the park's caves, found on the northeastern coast. Baranca Sunu, the so-called Tunnel of Love, has a heart-shape entrance and naturally sculpted rocks farther inside that some say look like the Madonna, Abe Lincoln, and even a jaguar. Guadirikiri Cave and Fontein Cave are marked with ancient drawings (rangers are on hand to offer explanations), as both were used by indigenous people centuries ago. Bats are known to make appearances—don't worry, they won't bother you. Although you don't need a flashlight because the paths are well lighted, it's best to wear sneakers.

11 **FRENCHMAN'S PASS.** Overhanging trees and towering cacti border this luscious stretch of road. The pass is almost midway between Oranjestad and San Nicolas; follow L. G. Smith Boulevard past a shimmering vista of blue-green sea and turn off where you see the drive-in theater (a popular local hangout). Then proceed to the first intersection, turn right, and follow the curve to the right. Gold was discovered on Aruba in 1824, and near Frenchman's Pass are the massive concrete-and-limestone ruins of the **Balashi Gold Smelter,** a lovely place to picnic and listen to the chattering parakeets. A magnificent, gnarled divi-divi tree guards the entrance. The area now is home to Aruba's desalination plant, where all of the island's drinking water is purified.

Cunucu Houses

Pastel houses surrounded by cacti fences adorn Aruba's flat, rugged cunucu ("country" in Papiamento). The features of these traditional houses were developed in response to the environment. Early settlers discovered that slanting roofs allowed the heat to rise and that small windows helped to keep in the cool air. Among the earliest building materials was caliche, a durable calcium-carbonate substance found in the island's southeastern hills. Many houses were also built using interlocking coral rocks that didn't require mortar (this technique is no longer used, thanks to cement and concrete). Contemporary design combines some of the basic principles of the earlier homes with touches of modernization: windows, though still narrow, have been elongated; roofs are constructed of bright tiles; pretty patios have been added; and doorways and balconies present an ornamental face to the world beyond.

⓭ **SAN NICOLAS.** During the heyday of the oil refineries, Aruba's oldest village was a bustling port; now its primary purpose is tourism. The institution in town is Charlie's Restaurant & Bar, a hangout for more than 50 years. Stop in for a drink and advice on what to see and do in this little town. The town is also home to Aruba's main red-light district, so there's plenty of street color.

⓬ **SAVANETA.** The Dutch settled here after retaking the island in 1816, and it served as Aruba's first capital. Today it's a bustling fishing village with a 150-year-old *cas de torto* (mud hut), the oldest dwelling still standing on the island.

⓮ **SEROE COLORADO.** What was originally built as a community for oil workers is known for its intriguing 1939 chapel. The site is surreal, as organ-pipe cacti form the backdrop for sedate whitewashed cottages. The real reason to come here is a **natural**

bridge. Keep bearing east past the community, continuing uphill until you run out of road. You can then hike down to the cathedral-like formation. It's not too strenuous, but watch your footing as you descend. Be sure to follow the white arrows painted on the rocks, as there are no other directional signs. Although this bridge isn't as spectacular as its more celebrated sibling (which collapsed in 2005), the raw elemental power of the sea that created it, replete with hissing blow holes, certainly is.

The young American couple entering Cuba's Cookin' seems momentarily stunned by the laughter and music. It's Saturday night in Oranjestad, and the tiny restaurant is filled with festive patrons drinking mojitos *and swaying to the music of a live band. The couple ponders a retreat back onto the busy street, but they decide to take the plunge and head toward the bar. Just half an hour later they are on the floor dancing, having learned an important lesson: in the battle between* mojitos *and inhibitions—*mojitos always *win.*

In This Chapter

nightlife

THEY PUMP UP THE VOLUME at Aruba's resort bars when the sun sets. Unlike many other islands, nightlife here isn't confined to touristy folkloric shows. In addition to spending time in one of the many casinos, you can slowly savor a drink while the sun dips into the sea, dance to the beat of a local band, bar-hop in a colorful bus, or simply stroll along a deserted starlit beach.

HOW & WHEN

Arubans like to party—the more the merrier—and they usually start celebrating late in the evening. The action, mostly on weekends, doesn't pick up until around midnight. Casual yet trendy attire is the norm. Most bars don't have a cover charge, although most nightclubs do. Bigger clubs, such as Club Havana, may have lines on weekends, but they move quickly; use this time to start your socializing and you may just end up with a dance partner before you even set foot inside the door. Drink specials are available at some bars, and every establishment will gladly give you a free Balashi Cocktail (the local term for a glass of water). Both bars and clubs have either live bands or DJs, depending on the night.

No matter where you choose to party, be smart about getting back to your hotel. Drinking and driving, of course, is against the law. If you're within walking distance, go ahead and hoof it. Taxis are a good option if your hotel is farther away. The island is safe, and you'll probably wander with swarms of other visitors in town and along Palm Beach.

A Bartender's Life

For some people, tending bar is a job. But for Tariq Ohab, one of Aruba's most popular bartenders, it's a way of life. Born in Aruba, the islander has a passion for mixing cocktails and everything that goes along with it. "If I could have any bartending job in the world," he says, "I'd like to stay right here."

Ohab lived in the United States for about eight years, but eventually moved back to the island he loves—a fact that endears him to his local clients, who appreciate his knowledge of Aruban culture and tales of his travels. Ohab recalls swapping small-world stories with a couple from Spokane who were surprised to find he had once lived in Olympia. "I meet a lot of interesting people," he says. "Most of the people I meet are always ready to start a conversation and chat up a storm."

Café Bahia, a popular watering hole, has been Ohab's habitat for the past eight years. Although most of his clients are tourists trying to take their minds off their sunburns, plenty of celebrities drop by for a cold one. Baseball player Sidney Ponson, a native of Aruba, is a regular. One day O. J. Simpson himself paid a visit. "He ordered orange juice," says Ohab, "and that's no joke."

Ohab especially enjoys mixing up Café Bahia's specialty drinks. The best bang for the buck, according to Ohab, is called the Blackout. "It's the strongest drink we have," he says. "It's made with five shots: tequila, whiskey, amaretto, 151, and Southern Comfort. It's topped with cranberry juice; then we mix in some blue grenadine, and it becomes black before your eyes." Served in a big glass, the concoction takes an average person about an hour to finish. Most customers, he adds, don't stop at just one.

It may sound like Ohab's life is one big party, but he has a mellower side as well. On Sunday, his day off, you'll find him at home with his wife and two kids. "Since my job is so social, I go out every night of the week," he says. "On Sundays, it's all about the family."

SOURCES

For information on specific events check out the free magazines *Aruba Nights*, *Aruba Events*, *Aruba Experience*, and *Aruba Holiday*, all available at the airport and at hotels.

Bar-Hopping Buses

A couple of bus operators can turn a regular evening out on the town into a whirlwind tour of the island's hottest nightspots. One uniquely Aruban institution is a psychedelically painted '57 Chevy bus called the **KUKOO KUNUKU** (tel. 297/586–2010, www.kukookunuku.com). Weeknights you'll find as many as 40 passengers traveling between half a dozen bars from sundown to around midnight. The $59 fee per passenger includes dinner, drinks, and picking you up (and pouring you out) at your hotel. Group and private charter rates are available. Needless to say, reservations are essential. **BANANA BUS** (www.bananabusaruba.com) offers a similar experience—minus dinner—in a bus with a 20-foot banana mounted on the roof. Five drinks are included in the $37-per-person price. Reservations can be made at your hotel front desk, and the bus will pick you up there as well.

Bars

Catch a glimpse of the elaborate swimming pool with whirlpools, waterslides, and waterfalls from the Hyatt Regency Aruba Beach Resort & Casino's **ALFRESCO LOBBY BAR** (J. E. Irausquin Blvd. 85, Palm Beach, tel. 297/586–1234 Ext. 4265) while sipping a fine wine or a tropical cocktail. This is where guests gather to hear live music early in the evening and stop by for a nightcap after the casino closes. Many visitors, including those on party buses, ★ find their way to **CARLOS & CHARLIE'S** (Weststraat 3A, Oranjestad, tel. 297/582–0355), which may be why locals shy away from it. You'll find mixed drinks by the yard, Mexican fare, and American music from the '60s, '70s, and '80s.

In business since 1948, **CHETA'S BAR** (Paradera 119, Paradera, tel. 297/582–3689) is a real local joint that holds no more than four customers at a time. There aren't any bar stools, either, which is why most patrons gather out front. There is always a lively crowd at the cozy **CUBA'S COOKIN'** (Wilhelminastraat 27, Oranjestad, tel. 297/588–0627), which also serves great ethnic food. On weekends the bar is packed with people who come to enjoy live Cuban music, and the dancing goes on until the wee hours of the morning. ★ You can watch the crowds from the terrace at **CHOOSE A NAME** (Havenstraat 36, Oranjestad, tel. 297/588–6200) or climb up on the bar for your karaoke debut. Bands perform several nights a week. Out in San Nicholas, **CHARLIE'S BAR** (Main St., San Nicholas, tel. 297/584-5086) is an Aruban institution that has been getting people tipsy since 1941. The bar initially catered to the rowdy crowd from the nearby refinery, but today Charlie's is crowded with tourists.

COCO BEACH BAR & GRILL RESTAURANT (Coco's Beach, Seroe Colorado, tel. 297/584–3434) is a popular spot for food and drinks any time of the day or night. For specialty drinks, try **IGUANA JOE'S** (Royal Plaza Mall, L. G. Smith Blvd. 94, Oranjestad, tel. 297/583–9373). The creative reptilian-theme decor is as colorful as the cocktails.

The beachfront **KOKOA BEACH BAR** (Palm Beach, tel. 297/586–2050) is often full of beauties in skimpy bathing suits and windsurfers in baggy shorts. There's live local music Friday and Sunday, with everything from reggae and salsa to pop. ★ With painted parrots flocking on the ceiling, **MAMBO JAMBO** (Royal Plaza Mall 126, L. G. Smith Blvd. 94, Oranjestad, tel. 297/583–3632) is daubed in sunset colors. Sip one of several concoctions sold nowhere else on the island, then browse for memorabilia at a shop next door.

With front-row seats to view the green flash—that ray of light that allegedly flicks through the sky as the sun sinks into the ocean—the **PALMS BAR** (Hyatt Regency Aruba Beach Resort & Casino,

Brewing Up Something Special

There was a time when you could walk into any bar in Aruba and get a glass of water by asking for a Balashi Cocktail. (The name came from the fact that the desalination plant is in an area known as Balashi.) Since the creation of Balashi, the first locally brewed beer, such a drink order has taken on a whole new meaning.

Made by a German brewmaster in a state-of-the-art facility using only the finest hops and malt, Balashi is golden-colored pilsner. The beer is a source of local pride, even more so since it won the prestigious Monde Selection at an international competition in 2001. Visitors love it as well. "It's a big tourist thing," explains Gerben Tilma, general manager of the plant. "Everyone wants to know what the best local products are. Now we can tell them."

The **BALASHI BREWERY** *(Balashi, tel. 297/585–4805) has a free one-hour tour at 10 AM daily. There's also a souvenir shop, a café, and a 10,000-square-foot beer garden where you can enjoy a cold one.*

J. E. Irausquin Blvd. 85, Palm Beach, tel. 297/586–1234) is the perfect spot to enjoy the sunset. At La Cabana All Suite Beach Resort & Casino, the **SUNSET BAR** (J. E. Irausquin Blvd. 250, Eagle Beach, tel. 297/587–9000) serves cocktails at the swim-up bar.

Cruises

On the **SUNSET HAPPY HOUR CRUISE** (tel. 297/586–2010), aboard the 80-foot sailing vessel *Mi Dushi*, you can enjoy Caribbean snacks as you toast with champagne. The open-air bar serves premium brands (included in your ticket price). Cruises depart Wednesday and Friday at 5 PM from the Aruba Grand Beach Resort Pier and return about 7 PM. The cost is $25 per person.

Don't be surprised if you're enjoying a romantic ocean-view dinner on Palm Beach and you see a twinkle of lights on the horizon. It may be the **TATTOO** (tel. 297/586–2010), a catamaran that sails every night except Sunday from 8 PM to midnight. It has three decks for dancing (there are live bands and a DJ), dining, and stargazing. End the evening with the famous rope swing and waterslide. The cost is $39 per person.

Dance & Music Clubs

★ Popular with locals and tourists, **CAFÉ BAHIA** (Weststraat 7, Oranjestad, tel. 297/588–9982) draws a chic crowd every Friday for happy hour. Come for dinner and stick around for drinking and dancing as the music heats up. Tuesday nights, a band from one of the cruise ships plays local favorites. The newest hot spot is **CLUB HAVANA** (L. G. Smith Boulevard 2, Oranjestad, tel. 297/582–0152), where the Friday happy hour lasts until 2 AM. Two local bands jam live on Saturday from 10 PM to 4 AM.

The energy doesn't diminish until closing time at **EUPHORIA** (Royal Plaza Mall, L. G. Smith Blvd. 93, Oranjestad), where a young crowd raves the night away. **LA FIESTA** (Aventura Mall, Plaza Daniel Leo, Oranjestad, tel. 297/583–5896) attracts a casual yet classy crowd. Inside, heavy red curtains add drama. Although there's no dance floor, a cool mix of music inspires patrons to bop at the bar.

Stop by the cozy **SIROCCO LOUNGE** (Wyndham Aruba Beach Resort & Casino, L. G. Smith Blvd. 77, Palm Beach, tel. 297/586–4466) for jazz every night except Sunday. ★ Try the cozy **GARUFA CIGAR & COCKTAIL LOUNGE** (Wilhelminastraat 63, Oranjestad, tel. 297/582–7205) for jazz and other types of music. It serves as a lounge for customers awaiting a table at the nearby El Gaucho Argentine Grill. While you wait, have a drink, enjoy some appetizers, and take in the leopard-print carpet and funky bar stools. The ambience may draw you back for an after-dinner cognac.

Local bands are always in the spotlight at the beachside **GILLIGAN'S** (Radisson Aruba Caribbean Resort, J. E. Irausquin

Cool Concoctions

These drink recipes come from Aruban-born bartender Clive Van Der Linde.

THE WOW. *Mix equal parts (2 ounces or so) of rum and vodka as well as triple sec, a splash of tequila, grenadine, coconut cream, and pineapple and orange juice. Quips Van Der Linde, "You won't taste the alcohol, but after two, you'll feel pretty good."*

THE IGUANA. *Mix equal parts of rum and vodka, and add either blue Curaçao or blue grenadine for color. Add crème de banana liqueur, coconut cream, and pineapple juice. Says Van Der Linde, "I learned this one more than 10 years ago on the first sailing boat I worked on. It was called the* Balia, *which means 'to dance.' "*

THE CAPTAIN'S SPECIAL. *Mix equal parts of rum and vodka, and add a splash of amaretto, crème de banana, and pineapple and orange juice. "It's really simple," says Van Der Linde. "Just blend with crushed ice and it's ready to drink."*

Blvd. 81, Palm Beach, tel. 297/586–6555). You'll feel like you've been shipwrecked on an uncharted tropical isle as you sip cocktails at the bar. Musicians take to the stage every evening at **PATA PATA** (La Cabana All Suite Beach Resort & Casino, J. E. Irausquin Blvd. 250, Eagle Beach, tel. 297/587–9000). Live music every evening makes **PELICAN TERRACE** (Divi Aruba Beach Resort, J. E. Irausquin Blvd. 45, Druif Beach, tel. 297/582–3300) a popular nightspot. Sip creative cocktails, dance around the pool, and grab a late-night snack—perhaps a pizza that's piping hot from the wood-burning oven. Liveliness is guaranteed, as most of the other patrons are resort guests enjoying all-inclusive drinks.

Local bands alternate sets at **RICK'S AMERICANA CAFÉ** (Wyndham Aruba Beach Resort & Casino, J. E. Irausquin Blvd.

77, Palm Beach, tel. 297/586–4466), a popular watering hole. The bar is inside the hotel's casino, so you can throw a quarter in the slots on your way in—you just might win enough to cover your bar tab. At the **STELLARIS LOUNGE & LOBBY BAR** (Aruba Marriott Resort & Stellaris Casino, L. G. Smith Blvd. 101, Palm Beach, tel. 297/586–9000) local bands gets the party started about 9 PM and keep it going till at least 2 AM.

Fun Without the Sun

At last count there were more than 50 theme nights offered during the course of a week. Each party features a buffet dinner, dancing, and entertainment (often of the limbo, steel-band, stilt-walking variety). For a complete list contact the Aruba Tourism Authority. The **ARUBA MARRIOTT** (L. G. Smith Blvd. 101, Palm Beach, tel. 297/586–9000) has a fun Carnival show on Tuesday night. One of the best theme parties is the **HAVANA TROPICAL** (Wyndham Aruba Beach Resort & Casino, J. E. Irausquin Blvd. 77, Palm Beach, tel. 297/586–4466), which rocks every night except Monday and Sunday. You can get your limbo on at the Wednesday party at the **HOLIDAY INN SUNSPREE** (J. E. Irausquin Blvd. 230, Palm Beach, tel. 297/586–3600).

Movies

With six screens, **SEAPORT CINEMA** (Seaport Market Pl., tel. 297/583–0318) has all the latest American movies. The earliest shows are around 4 PM; late shows start around 10:30 PM during the week and midnight on weekends. Ticket prices range from about $6 to $7.

Check out the not-so-silver screen under the stars at the **E. DE VEER DRIVE-IN THEATER** (Kibaima z/n, across the road from the Balashi Brewery, Santa Cruz, tel. 297/585–8355). It will cost you about $3 to watch the English-language movies on this massive screen. Movies start at 8:30 PM. The drive-in can accommodate about 100 cars and has a snack bar.

Temperature & Liquid Volume Conversion Chart

Temperature: Metric Conversions

To change Centigrade or Celsius (C) to Fahrenheit (F), multiply C by 1.8 and add 32. To change F to C, subtract 32 from F and multiply by .555.

F°	C°	F°	C°
0	-17.8	60	15.5
10	-12.2	70	21.1
20	-6.7	80	26.6
30	-1.1	90	32.2
32	0	98.6	37.0
40	+4.4	100	37.7
50	10.0		

Liquid Volume: Liters/U.S. Gallons

To change liters (L) to U.S. gallons (gal), multiply L by .264. To change U.S. gal to L, multiply gal by 3.79.

L to gal	gal to L
1 = .26	1 = 3.8
2 = .53	2 = 7.6
3 = .79	3 = 11.4
4 = 1.1	4 = 15.2
5 = 1.3	5 = 19.0
6 = 1.6	6 = 22.7
7 = 1.8	7 = 26.5
8 = 2.1	8 = 30.3

It's Tuesday night at the Bon Bini Festival. Performers run onto the stage as steel-pan drummers pound out a heart-racing beat. The rhythm prompts a local dance troupe to converge on the scene; the audience is mesmerized by their traditional movements and colorful costumes. One observer, an island visitor, gets up and joins the dance. A local man with a bead of sweat on his brow flashes her a bright smile and says, "Hey, you ever seen this before? This is the good stuff."

In This Chapter

the arts

PUERTO RICO HAS RICKY MARTIN, Jamaica has Bob Marley, and Aruba has . . . well, Aruba has a handful of stars who aren't quite as famous but are just as talented. Over the years, several local artists, including composer Julio Renado Euson (who once won a competition against Ricky Martin), choreographer Wilma Kuiperi, sculptor Ciro Abath, and visual artist Elvis Lopez, have gained international renown. Further, many Aruban musicians play more than one type of music (classical, jazz, soca, salsa, reggae, calypso, rap, pop), and many compose as well as perform.

The Union of Cultural Organizations is devoted to developing local art while broadening its international appeal. UNOCA provides scholarships to help artists of all ages to participate in exhibitions, shows, and festivals. Although some internationally recognized stars have returned to Aruba to help promote the island's cultural growth, renowned conductor and pianist Eldin Juddan says the island needs to do more to promote local musicians. "There's a lot of talent, but professional guidance is needed to bring these talents and music to their potential."

The **CAS DI CULTURA** (Vondellaan 2, Oranjestad, tel. 297/582–1010), the island's cultural center, continuously hosts art exhibits, folkloric shows, dance performances, and concerts. Further, the island's many festivals showcase arts and culture. To find out what's going on, check out *Aruba Today*, the local newspaper, or *Calalou*, a Caribbean publication dedicated to the visual arts. You can also phone the national library, which has a bulletin board of events.

In Tune with Jonathan Vieira

His parents were always traveling, so when musician Jonathan Vieira was growing up, he often stayed with his grandmother. He was fascinated with her old piano. He hit his first note when he was four, and has been playing ever since. The Aruba native, who taught himself to play, recorded an album called Two Generations *with Padu del Caribe, one of the composers of the island's national anthem. Vieira speaks highly of his collaborator, calling him the "father of our culture."*

"On Aruba, people need to have more of an awareness of cultural music," Vieira says. "The popular stuff catches on quick; we have to have a balance." Many of his own musical creations show his affinity for local rhythms, though he also is well versed in classical and contemporary music.

When he was about 14, a local promoter heard about his talents and invited him to open one of the concerts she was organizing. The reaction was positive, and for the first time Vieira realized he could use his talent to make some money—or at least pay his school expenses. At age 17, Vieira headed to the United States to continue his education. He attended the Berkeley College of Business in New York City, where he earned a degree in information management systems. It was his third degree; the others are in film and video production and recording arts production. "On the island," says Vieira, "everyone knows me as a pianist."

Although his first love is music, Vieira has also been dabbling in film. "I have been doing a bit of acting recently to try it out," he says. In the meantime, Vieira is busy giving back to the island he calls home. He returns to Aruba in the summer to give chamber concerts at the Access, an art gallery and performance space in Oranjestad. He also invites other artists to join him in special holiday performances.

ART GALLERIES

★ **ACCESS GALLERY.** Showcasing new and established artists, this gallery is a major venue for Caribbean art. Located in the downtown shopping district, it is home to a thriving cultural scene that includes poetry readings, chamber-music concerts, and screenings of feature films and documentaries. *Caya Betico Croes 16–18, Oranjestad, tel. 297/588–7837.*

GALERIA ETERNO. At this gallery you'll find local and international artists at work. Be sure to stop by for concerts by classical guitarists, dance performances, visual-arts shows, and plays. *Emanstraat 92, Oranjestad, tel. 297/583–9607.*

GALERIA HARMONIA. The island's largest gallery has changing art exhibits as well as a permanent collection of works by local and international artists. *Zeppenfeldstraat 10, San Nicolas, tel. 297/584–2969.*

GASPARITO RESTAURANT & ART GALLERY. This exceptional dining spot features an ongoing exhibition of works by Aruban artists. *Gasparito 3, Noord, tel. 297/586–7044.*

★ **INSIGHT ART STUDIO.** This contemporary gallery hosts exhibitions of local and international artists. Don't expect to find the usual paintings of pastel-colored skies. Owner Alida Martinez, a Venezuelan-born artist, likes more avant-garde displays. Her own mixed-medium creations juxtapose erotic and religious themes. The space, which includes a studio, is a magnet for the island's art community. Viewing is by appointment only. *Paradera Park 215, Paradera, tel. 297/582–5882.*

FESTIVALS

Annual Events

★ **THE DANDE STROLL.** New Year's Eve is a big deal in most places, but on Aruba, the fireworks that light up the sky at midnight are just the beginning. Celebrations continue throughout New

Year's Day. Groups of musicians stroll from house to house, singing good-luck greetings for the New Year. A prize is awarded to the group with the best song, which is sung by islanders during the next 12 months. Dande, by the way, comes from the Papiamento word "dandara," which means "to have a good time."

INTERNATIONAL DANCE FESTIVAL ARUBA. Each October, dance companies from the Caribbean, the United States, and Europe participate in workshops, lectures, demonstrations, and exhibitions.

INTERNATIONAL THEATRE FESTIVAL ARUBA. Every other October, theater groups from around the world perform 45- to 70-minute shows at the Cas Di Cultura.

JAZZ AND LATIN MUSIC FESTIVAL. For a few nights each June, you can hear jazz and Latin music performed at the outdoor venue next to the Renaissance Aruba Beach Resort at Seaport Village.

HI-WINDS PRO AM WINDSURFING COMPETITION. Windsurfers of all skill levels come from more than 30 different countries during June or July to compete off the beaches at Fisherman's Huts at Hadikurari.

NATIONAL ANTHEM & FLAG DAY. On this official holiday, held March 18, you can stop by Plaza Betico Croes in Oranjestad for folkloric presentations and other traditional festivities.

ARUBA MUSIC FESTIVAL. This two-day event held in September or October features international pop stars. (Sure, the artists may not have current hits, but the festival can be a fun nostalgic experience.) Past performers include Peter Frampton; Crosby, Stills & Nash; and Pat Benatar.

ST. JOHN'S DAY. Dera Gai, the annual "burying of the rooster" festival, is celebrated June 24, the Feast of St. John the Baptist.

Carnival

Aruba's biggest bash incorporates local traditions with those of Venezuela, Brazil, Holland, and North America. The festival was introduced to the island by Trinidadians who had come to work at the oil refinery in the 1940s. In Aruba, Carnival consists of six weeks of jump-ups (traditional Caribbean street celebrations), competitions, parties, and colorful parades. The celebrations culminate with the Grand Parade held in Oranjestad on the Sunday before Ash Wednesday. It lasts for hours and turns the streets into one big stage. The two main events are the Grand Children's Parade, where kids dress in colorful costumes and decorate floats, and the Lightning Parade, consisting of miles of glittery floats and lavish costumes. Steel-pan and brass bands supply the music that inspires the crowds to dance. All events end on Shrove Tuesday: at midnight an effigy of King Momo (traditionally depicted as a fat man) is burned, indicating the end of joy and the beginning of Lenten penitence.

Festive songs, bright yellow-and-red costumes, and traditional dances mark this holiday dating from 1862. Today, the rooster—which symbolizes a successful harvest—has been replaced by a gourd.

Weekly Parties

★ **BON BINI FESTIVAL.** The name of this year-round folkloric event means "welcome" in Papiamento; it's held every Tuesday from 6:30 PM to 8:30 PM at Oranjestad's historic Fort Zoutman. In the inner courtyard you can check out the Antillean dancers in resplendent costumes, feel the rhythms of the steel drums, browse among the stands displaying local artwork, and partake of local food and drink. Admission is $3.

A visitor from the United States became frustrated when he couldn't get in touch with his family—either via the Internet or his long-distance phone service—from his hotel. Another hotelier overheard the visitor complain about the problem to a beach buddy. The hotelier immediately offered to let the visitor use the facilities at his hotel, handing over a key to the private computer room. And, of course, the hotelier also invited the visitor to join him for coffee.

In This Chapter

where to stay

"CUIDA NOS TURISTA" ("TAKE CARE OF OUR TOURISTS") is the island's motto, and Arubans are taught the finer points of hospitality as soon as they learn to read and write. With such cordial hosts, it's hard to go wrong no matter which accommodation you choose.

Most hotels are west of Oranjestad, along L. G. Smith and J. E. Irausquin boulevards. Many are self-contained complexes, with restaurants, shops, casinos, water-sports centers, health clubs, and car-rental and travel desks. Room service, laundry and dry-cleaning services, in-room safes, minibars or refrigerators, and babysitting are standard at all but the smallest properties. Most places don't include meals in their rates. Still, you can shop around for good dining options, as hotel restaurants and clubs are open to all island guests.

Many people prefer to stay in time-shares, returning year after year and making the island a kind of home away from home. Some time-share patrons say they like the spacious, homey accommodations and the opportunity to prepare their own meals. Note that hotel-type amenities such as shampoo, hair dryers, and housekeeping service may not be offered in time-shares; if they are, they often cost extra. Time-shares and hotels typically charge a combined total of 19% taxes and service charges on top of quoted rates, so be sure to ask about taxes before booking to avoid sticker-shock when you check out.

lodging

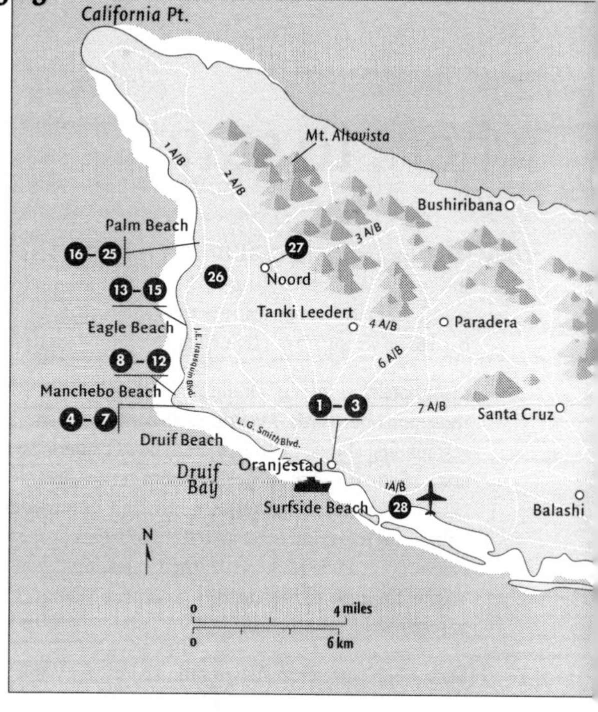

Amsterdam Manor Beach Resort, **14**

Aruba Beach Club, **12**

Aruba Divi Phoenix Beach Resort, **23**

Aruba Marriott Resort & Stellaris Casino, **18**

Boardwalk Vacation Retreat, **16**

Brickell Bay Beach Club, **25**

Bucuti Beach Resort, **10**

La Cabana All Suite Beach Resort & Casino, **15**

Caribbean Palm Village, **27**

Casa Del Mar Beach Resort, **3**

Costa Linda Beach Resort, **8**

Divi Aruba Beach Resort Mega All Inclusive, **5**

Divi Dutch Village, **7**

Divi Village Golf & Beach Resort, **6**

Holiday Inn SunSpree Aruba Beach Resort & Casino, **21**

Hyatt Regency Aruba Beach Resort & Casino, **19**

Manchebo Beach Resort & Spa, **11**

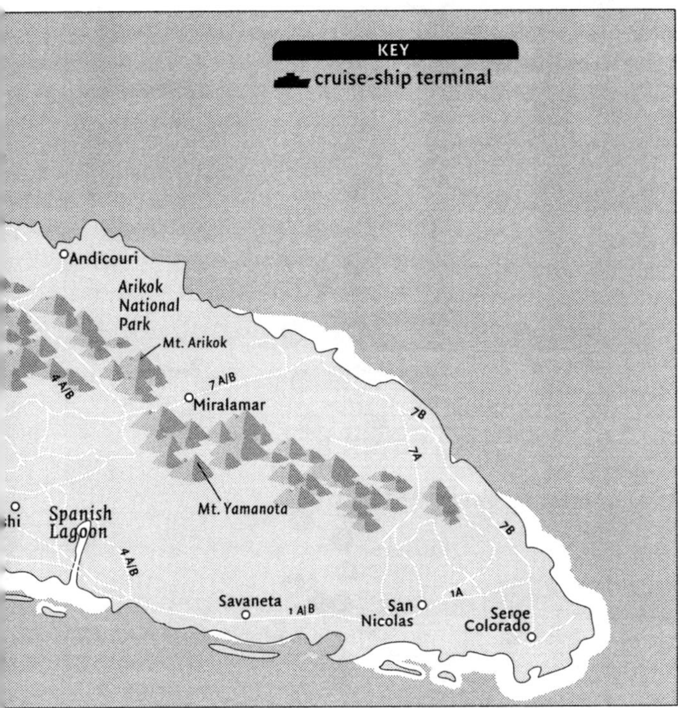

Marriott's Aruba Ocean Club, **17**

Mill Resort & Suites, **26**

MVC Eagle Beach, **13**

Playa Linda Beach Resort, **24**

La Quinta Beach Resort, **9**

Radisson Aruba Resort & Casino, **22**

Renaissance Aruba Beach Resort & Casino, **1**

Talk of the Town Hotel & Beach Club, **2**

Tamarijn Aruba All Inclusive Beach Resort, **4**

Vistalmar, **28**

Wyndham Aruba Beach Resort & Casino, **20**

western aruba lodging

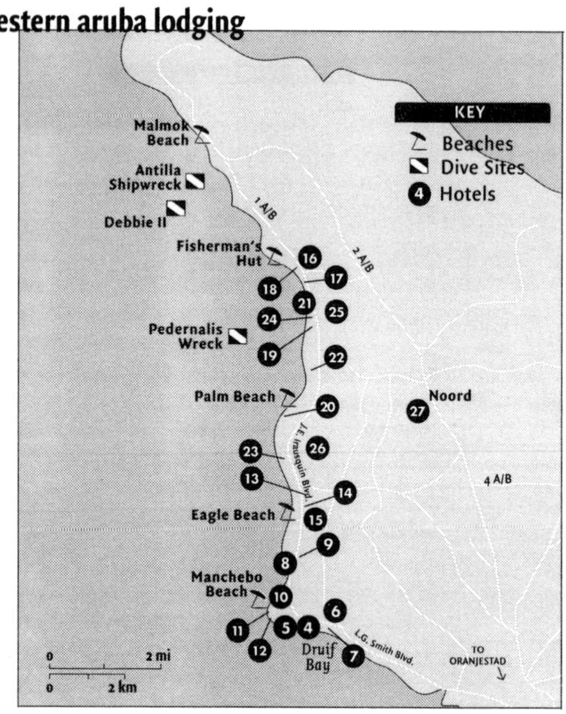

Amsterdam Manor Beach Resort, **14**

Aruba Beach Club, **12**

Aruba Divi Phoenix Beach Resort, **23**

Aruba Marriott Resort & Stellaris Casino, **18**

Boardwalk Vacation Retreat, **16**

Brickell Bay Beach Club, **25**

Bucuti Beach Resort, **10**

La Cabana All Suite Beach Resort & Casino, **15**

Caribbean Palm Village, **27**

Costa Linda Beach Resort, **8**

Divi Aruba Beach Resort Mega All Inclusive, **5**

Divi Dutch Village, **7**

Divi Village Golf & Beach Resort, **6**

Holiday Inn SunSpree Aruba Beach Resort & Casino, **21**

Hyatt Regency Aruba Beach Resort & Casino, **19**

Manchebo Beach Resort & Spa, **11**

Marriott's Aruba Ocean Club, **17**

Mill Resort & Suites, **26**

MVC Eagle Beach, **13**

Playa Linda Beach Resort, **24**

La Quinta Beach Resort, **9**

Radisson Aruba Resort & Casino, **22**

Tamarijn Aruba All Inclusive Beach Resort, **4**

Wyndham Aruba Beach Resort & Casino, **20**

Prices

Hotel rates are high; to save money, take advantage of airline and hotel packages, or visit during the summer when rates are discounted by as much as 40%. If you're traveling with kids, ask about discounts; children often stay for free in their parents' room, though there are age cutoffs. Prices are in U.S. dollars.

CATEGORY	HOTELS EP,BP, CP	HOTELS AI
$$$$	over $350	over $450
$$$	$250–$350	$350–$450
$$	$150–$250	$250–$350
$	$80–$150	$125–$250
¢	under $80	under $125

Prices are for two people in a standard double room in high season, excluding 8% taxes and 11% service charges.

$$$$ ★ **ARUBA MARRIOTT RESORT & STELLARIS CASINO.** Located in the heart of the high-rise area, this resort has it all. Rooms have large balconies, and most have delightful ocean views. The grounds are beautifully landscaped and lead directly to the beach. It feels like there is always something going on here, from dramatic live shows to more relaxed theme nights. Tuscany, the respected Italian restaurant, is one of the most romantic dining spots on the island. There are also numerous dining choices within walking distance. High and low rollers alike will appreciate the convenience of having one of the island's larger casinos on the premises. Express checkout is available. *L. G. Smith Blvd. 101, Palm Beach, tel. 297/586–9000 or 800/223–6388, fax 297/586–0649. www.marriott.com. 375 rooms, 35 suites. 5 restaurants, café, in-room safes, minibars, cable TV with movies, in-room VCRs, in-room data ports, Wi-Fi, 2 tennis courts, pool, fitness classes, health club, hair salon, massage, sauna, spa, beach, dive shop, windsurfing, boating, jet skiing, volleyball, 4 bars, casino, shops, concierge, Internet, meeting rooms, car rental. AE, D, DC, MC, V. EP.*

Associations That Accommodate

The **ARUBA HOTEL & TOURISM ASSOCIATION** *(tel. 297/582–2607, www.ahata.com) was established in 1965 to maintain high standards in the tourism industry. From its original seven hotels, the organization has grown into a powerhouse of more than 80 businesses, including restaurants, casinos, stores, tour operators, and airlines. The organization's $4 million annual budget, earmarked to promote Aruba as a travel destination, comes from the Aruba Tourism Authority and from private-sector partners. You can express opinions and register complaints on the Aruba Tourism Web site, www.aruba.com. The organization is also involved in anti-litter efforts as part of the Aruba Limpi Committee.*

Another association, the **ARUBA APARTMENT RESORT & SMALL HOTEL ASSOCIATION** *(tel. 297/582–3289), represents smaller, less expensive hotels. Members are expected to meet certain standards of accommodations and service and still offer affordable rates (often as low as $65 per night).*

$$$$ ★ HYATT REGENCY ARUBA BEACH RESORT & CASINO. Hacienda-roofed buildings make this property a landmark in the high-rise hotel area. Beach access and spa services make it easy to relax. Kids love the massive pool and the Camp Hyatt program that teaches them Aruban-style storytelling, Caribbean cooking, and arts and crafts. Relax on the beach, play tennis, or go horseback riding before an afternoon hydrotherapy treatment. Ruinas del Mar serves continental fare, and Japengo is known for seafood with an Asian flair. At the time of this writing, the resort was beginning a $20 million renovation; work is scheduled to be completed by Spring 2007. *J. E. Irausquin Blvd. 85, Palm Beach, tel. 297/586–1234 or 800/554–9288, fax 297/586–5478. www.hyatt.com. 342 rooms, 18 suites. 5 restaurants, snack bar, room service, fans, in-room safes, minibars, cable TV with movies, 2 tennis courts, pool, health club,* *hair salon, 2 outdoor hot tubs, massage, sauna, spa, steam room, beach, dive shop, dock, snorkeling, windsurfing, boating, jet skiing, waterskiing, basketball, horseback riding, volleyball, 5 bars, casino, shops, babysitting, children's programs (ages 3–12), playground, concierge, Internet, business services, car rental, travel services.* AE, D, DC, MC, V. EP.

$$$$ ★ **MARRIOTT'S ARUBA OCEAN CLUB.** First-rate amenities and lavishly decorated villas have made this time-share the talk of the island. Each one- and two-bedroom unit includes a kitchen and a balcony with a spectacular ocean view. The S-shape pool has a swim-up bar and waterfalls; there are four hot tubs built into the rocks above. You can access the facilities at the adjacent Aruba Marriott Resort & Stellaris Casino, including the spa, fitness center, and casino. An adjacent time-share property, Marriott's Aruba Surf Club, is just as luxurious. *L. G. Smith Blvd. 99, Palm Beach, tel. 297/586–2641, fax 297/586–8000. www.marriott.com. 218 units. Restaurant, grocery, kitchenettes, microwaves, refrigerators, cable TV with movies, pool, spa, beach, dive shop, snorkeling, windsurfing, boating, jet skiing, shops, Internet, meeting rooms.* AE, D, DC, MC, V. EP.

$$$$ ★ **RADISSON ARUBA RESORT & CASINO.** This resort—one of the largest on the island—is devoted to pampering its guests. Exquisitely manicured grounds (complete with waterfalls) merge seamlessly with the beach. The stone floor lobby features friendly resident macaws and parrots that seem eager for a photo opportunity. Rooms are large, and all feature handsome four-poster colonial-style beds. The designers thought of everything: blue accent lighting, wood furniture on the balconies, and plantation shutters. Unwind in the fitness center or spa, then enjoy a meal at one of the hotel's excellent restaurants. Try Gilligan's at the beach for simple fare, or the Sunset Grille for more elaborate dishes. *J. E. Irausquin Blvd. 81, Palm Beach, tel. 297/586–6555, fax 297/586–3260. www.radisson.com. 358 rooms, 32 suites. 4 restaurants, room service, in-room safes, minibars, cable TV with movies, golf privileges, 2 tennis courts, 2 pools, health club, spa, beach, dive shop, snorkeling,* *boating, jet skiing, 3 bars, video game room, babysitting, children's programs (ages 5–12), dry cleaning, laundry service, Internet, business services, convention center, meeting rooms.* AE, D, DC, MC, V. BP.

$$$–$$$$ **COSTA LINDA BEACH RESORT.** The name of this hotel, Spanish for "beautiful coast," speaks for itself. This paradise on earth is spread along a pristine 600-foot stretch of Eagle Beach. An inviting blue pool sits in the center of the manicured grounds. Pamper yourself with numerous amenities in the bright, spacious two-bedroom suites, which include Roman tubs and balconies overlooking the crystalline sea. Larger units also have outdoor hot tubs and barbecue grills. There are lighted tennis courts on the premises, and scuba diving, snorkeling, and boating opportunities nearby. In the evening, take a stroll to the nearby Alhambra Casino. *J. E. Irausquin Blvd. 59, Eagle Beach, tel. 297/583–8000, fax 297/583–6040. www.costalinda-aruba.com. 155 suites. 2 restaurants, kitchenettes, refrigerators, cable TV, 2 tennis courts, pool, wading pool, health club, 2 bars, shops, babysitting, children's programs (ages 5–12), dry cleaning, laundry facilities, Internet.* AE, MC, V. EP.

$$$–$$$$ **DIVI ARUBA BEACH RESORT MEGA ALL INCLUSIVE.** At this Mediterranean-style resort, you have your choice of standard rooms, beachfront lanais, or casitas that overlook courtyards and are often only steps from the beach. The mint-and-jade color scheme and white-tile floors are soothing. Make your own strawberry daiquiri and order piping hot pizzas at the poolside Pelican Bar. You can also dine and use the facilities at the adjacent Tamarijn Aruba All Inclusive Beach Resort. The rate includes non-motorized water sports and all food and drinks, but it does not cover expenses such as spa treatments or babysitting. Guest have access to the facilities of all Divi resorts on Aruba. *L. G. Smith Blvd. 93, Druif Beach, tel. 297/582–3300 or 800/554–2008, fax 297/583–1940. www.diviaruba.com. 203 rooms, 20 lanais, 42 casitas. 5 restaurants, fans, refrigerators, cable TV, golf privileges, tennis court, 2 pools, gym, hair salon, outdoor hot tub, beach, dive shop, snorkeling, windsurfing, boating, waterskiing, bicycles, shuffleboard, volleyball, 3 bars, shops, babysitting, laundry service, Internet.* AE, D, DC, MC, V. AI.

$$$–$$$$ **PLAYA LINDA BEACH RESORT.** Set on one of the nicest sections of Eagle Beach, this lovely resort is constructed like a stepped Mayan pyramid. The design allows for maximum visibility from individual rooms and means that most balconies open to the sky. All units are fully equipped with kitchens—a great money-saving feature for families. Spacious studios and one- and two-bedroom suites are lavishly appointed. Frolic on the beach, dip in the free-form pool or one of the hot tubs, play a few games of tennis, or shop in the arcade. In the evening, you can watch the sunset from the terrace or hit the free weekly cocktail party. Come morning, grab a quick bite at on-site Dushi Bagels. If you're looking for one of the best views on the island and a massive balcony, complete with barbecue and hot tub, consider a penthouse suite. *J. E. Irausquin Blvd. 87, Palm Beach, tel. 297/586–1000, fax 297/586–5210. www.playalinda.com. 203 units, 66 studios, 95 1-bedroom suites, 33 2-bedroom suites. Restaurant, in-room safes, kitchenettes, refrigerators, cable TV, putting green, 3 tennis courts, pool, health club, hot tub, beach, dive shop, windsurfing, boating, fishing, 2 bars, video game room, shops, babysitting, laundry facilities, Internet, meeting rooms. AE, D, DC, MC, V. CP.*

$$$–$$$$ **RENAISSANCE ARUBA BEACH RESORT & CASINO.** No other hotel on the island is closer to the heart of the downtown action. Shopping, nightlife, and numerous fine dining choices are minutes away. The hotel is not on the beach—but getting there is as simple as taking a boat from the lobby to the nearby private island. Rooms have all the amenities one would expect at a Renaissance hotel, and even those overlooking the huge hotel atrium are completely insulated from noise. At the lobby pool, you can lounge in the sun while watching the crowds 20 feet below on Oranjestad's main drag (you aren't visible to them, though). The hotel spa is one of the island's best. Rooms in the Marina section of the hotel are a bit further from the action but offer better ocean views. *L. G. Smith Blvd. 82, Oranjestad, tel. 297/583–6000 or 800/766–3782, fax 297/582–5317. www.arubarenaissance.com. 544 rooms, 15 suites. 5 restaurants, room service, kitchenettes, minibars, some microwaves, cable TV with movies,* *golf privileges, tennis court, 3 pools, 2 gyms, massage, spa, beach, dive shop, snorkeling, marina, fishing, volleyball, 5 bars, 2 casinos, nightclub, video game room, shops, children's programs (ages 5–12), playground, laundry facilities, concierge, Internet, convention center, meeting rooms, no-smoking rooms. AE, D, DC, MC, V. EP.*

$$–$$$$ CASA DEL MAR BEACH RESORT. This beachside resort offers two parts recreation, one part rest and relaxation. Deluxe accommodations are quite comfortable, with amenities such as balconies and fully equipped kitchens. Play tennis on one of four lighted courts, work out in the exercise room, arrange water sports at the activities desk, or kick back with a book from the library. Dine poolside at the Calypso restaurant. Kids enjoy the special programs offered most weekdays from approximately 10:30 to noon. *L. G. Smith Blvd. 53, Punta Brabo Beach, tel. 297/582–3000 or 297/582–7000, fax 297/582–9044. www.casadelmar-aruba.com. 147 suites. Restaurant, grocery, in-room safes, kitchenettes, refrigerators, cable TV with movies, 4 tennis courts, pool, wading pool, hair salon, hot tub, beach, bar, library, video game room, shops, children's programs (ages 4–10), laundry facilities, Internet, car rental, travel services. AE, D, DC, MC, V. EP.*

$$$ ★ BUCUTI BEACH RESORT. On the widest, most secluded section of Eagle Beach, this European-style resort is a cut above the rest. Hacienda-style buildings house sunny rooms with cherrywood furnishings, sparkling tile floors, and ocean-view terraces. Extras include coffeemakers, microwaves, and hair dryers. The new oceanfront Tara Wing, with its chic rooms and soothing spa, proved so popular that the other guest rooms have been remodeled to match. Work out in the open-air fitness pavilion surrounded by lush gardens. Revel in 24-hour Internet access and wireless broadband connection throughout the resort—even on the beach. The hotel consistently wins awards for being environmentally conscientious. Book early, as repeat guests flood the resort every high season. *L. G. Smith Blvd. 55-B, Eagle Beach, tel. 297/583–1100, fax 297/582–5272. www.bucuti.com. 59 rooms, 42 suites, 3 bungalows.*

Restaurant, grocery, fans, in-room safes, minibars, microwaves, refrigerators, cable TV, Wi-Fi, pool, beach, bicycles, 2 bars, shop, laundry facilities, business services, travel services. AE, D, DC, MC, V. CP.

$$$ DIVI VILLAGE GOLF & BEACH RESORT. The newest of the mid-size Divi resorts focuses on golf, and although it's just across the road from its sister properties, the atmosphere is quieter and more refined. Another difference at this all-suites resort is the pricing structure; base rates are not all-inclusive, though you can purchase an AI plan that allows you to dine at the Divi Aruba and Tamarijn. Suites are massive and include kitchens; the beach is just across the road. Those seeking the ultimate in luxury can book one of the golf villas (with rooftop Jacuzzis) that overlook the links. The hotel grounds are as lush and well-maintained as the 9-hole golf course. Guest have access to the facilities of all Divi resorts on Aruba. *J. E. Irausquin Blvd. 47, Oranjestad, tel. 297/583–5000 or 800/367–3484, fax 297/582–0501. www.diviresorts.com.* 153 units. *Restaurant, kitchens, microwaves, refrigerators, cable TV, golf privileges, tennis court, bar.* AE, DC, MC, V. EP.

$$$ LA CABANA ALL SUITE BEACH RESORT & CASINO. This sprawling complex of high-rise buildings offers convenience and a good location at the expense of intimacy. It may feel more like an urban housing complex than a beach resort, but the key here is the availability of numerous services, restaurants, and diversions. The excellent Club Cabana Nana kid's program makes this a popular choice for families. A high occupancy level (time-shares make up much of the resort) means that the lively bars and restaurants are great places for meeting new people. The downside is that the pool area is normally packed, and you're unlikely to find peace and quiet here. About a third of the studios and one-bedroom suites have ocean views. All have kitchenettes, balconies, and hot tubs. Pricier villas are away from the main building. Planning to do your own cooking? You can order groceries online up to two days before your trip and have them delivered when you arrive. No need to bring a laptop; rent one for $25 a day, and get *wireless Internet access for about $15 per day. J. E. Irausquin Blvd. 250, Eagle Beach, tel. 297/587–9000 or 800/835–7193, fax 297/587–0844. www.lacabana.com. 811 suites. 3 restaurants, grocery, ice-cream parlor, in-room safes, kitchenettes, microwaves, cable TV, 5 tennis courts, 3 pools, fitness classes, health club, 3 outdoor hot tubs, massage, sauna, spa, dive shop, basketball, racquetball, shuffleboard, squash, volleyball, 5 bars, video game room, shops, playground, Internet, meeting rooms.* AE, D, DC, MC, V. EP.

$$$ TAMARIJN ARUBA ALL INCLUSIVE BEACH RESORT. Part of the Divi complex on lovely Druif Beach, this resort's two-story buildings stretch along the shore. Rooms all have beach views and simple, tasteful rattan and wicker furnishings. The large balconies are great places to enjoy the sunset or spend some quiet time. Although the pace here is quite slow, the animation of the adjoining Divi Aruba Beach Resort Mega All Inclusive is just a short walk away. In back of the buildings there are lush areas for sunning and relaxing. The rate covers food, beverages, entertainment, an array of activities, and even tickets to the weekly Bon Bini Festival. A bar at one end of the property serves food and drinks as a convenience for guests more removed from the main restaurants. A free shuttle runs to the Alhambra Casino until 3 AM. Guest have access to the facilities of all Divi resorts on Aruba. *J. E. Irausquin Blvd. 41, Druif Beach, tel. 297/582–4150 or 800/554–2008, fax 297/525–5203. www.tamarijnaruba.com. 236 rooms. 3 restaurants, snack bar, fans, cable TV, golf privileges, 2 tennis courts, 2 pools, health club, beach, snorkeling, windsurfing, boating, waterskiing, fishing, bicycles, Ping-Pong, shuffleboard, volleyball, 2 bars, shops, Internet, meeting rooms, car rental.* AE, D, DC, MC, V. AI.

$$$ WYNDHAM ARUBA BEACH RESORT & CASINO. From exciting windsurfing to sizzling nightlife, the Wyndham has something for everyone. Grand public spaces accommodate groups from North and South America, which make up most of the clientele. Rooms have mustard-color walls and handsome wood furniture. All have ocean-view balconies and amenities such as coffeemakers, minibars, and hair dryers. A "pool concierge" makes the rounds with magazines and CD players, and attendants spritz you with Evian, offer chilled towels, and serve frozen drinks. Treat yourself to a massage at the spa, just steps from the sand, and then to dinner at one of the upscale restaurants, ending the evening with a cocktail at the Sirocco Lounge. *J. E. Irausquin Blvd. 77, Palm Beach, tel. 297/586–4466 or 800/996–3426, fax 297/586–8217. www.wyndham.com. 481 rooms, 81 suites. 8 restaurants, in-room safes, minibars, cable TV, Wi-Fi, tennis court, pool, wading pool, hair salon, 2 outdoor hot tubs, spa, beach, dive shop, snorkeling, windsurfing, boating, jet skiing, parasailing, waterskiing, 4 bars, casino, video game room, shops, concierge, Internet, convention center.* AE, D, DC, MC, V. EP.

$$–$$$ **ARUBA BEACH CLUB.** Colonial charm and Dutch hospitality create an ambience that keeps families coming back year after year. All studios and one-bedroom units in this time-share property have bamboo furniture, satellite TVs, and balconies, sometimes with ocean views. There's plenty to do here, including yoga and language courses in Papiamento. The front desk can arrange for water sports and other activities. Kids enjoy the playground and their own pool. A shopping arcade is filled with boutiques, a frozen-yogurt shop, and a cybercafé. If all this isn't enough, you can use the facilities at the adjoining Casa del Mar Beach Resort. *J. E. Irausquin Blvd. 51–53, Punta Brabo Beach, tel. 297/582–3000, fax 297/582–6557. www.arubaonline.com/beachclub. 89 rooms, 42 suites. Restaurant, café, grocery, in-room safes, some kitchenettes, cable TV, 2 tennis courts, pool, wading pool, health club, hair salon, bar, video game room, shops, babysitting, children's programs (ages 3–12), playground, laundry service, Internet, meeting rooms, car rental, travel services.* AE, D, DC, MC, V. EP.

$$–$$$ **ARUBA DIVI PHOENIX BEACH RESORT.** A breathtaking location, a lively atmosphere, and comparatively reasonable rates make this hotel justifiably popular. Most of the studio and one- or two-bedroom units have balconies with ocean views. Tropical color schemes, wood furnishings, and lots of plants make you feel at home. Coffeemakers, microwaves, and hair dryers are among the thoughtful touches. Some rooms are wheelchair accessible. Sunset Beach Bistro serves breakfast, lunch, and dinner either indoors or on the beach. Work it off in the state-of-the-art fitness center. In the evening, enjoy live entertainment or try your luck at the nearby Alhambra Casino. Guest have access to the facilities of all Divi resorts on Aruba. *J. E. Irausquin Blvd. 75, Palm Beach, tel. 297/586–1170, fax 297/586–1165. www.diviarubaphoenix.com. 101 units, 36 studios, 56 1-bedroom suites, 9 2-bedroom suites. Restaurant, grocery, snack bar, fans, in-room safes, kitchenettes, microwaves, refrigerators, cable TV, in-room VCRs, golf privileges, pool, health club, hot tub, beach, snorkeling, boating, volleyball, 2 bars, shop, children's programs (ages 5–13), Internet, meeting rooms, travel services.* AE, D, DC, MC, V. EP.

$$ ★ **AMSTERDAM MANOR BEACH RESORT.** An intimate, family-run hotel with a genuinely friendly staff and an authentic Dutch-Caribbean atmosphere, this little place offers an excellent value for the money. The gabled mustard-yellow hotel is built around a central courtyard with a waterfall and wading pool. Eagle Beach is right across the road (guests can have lunch served on the beach). The pool bar is buzzing late into the night, and Filo, the bartender, keeps everyone entertained. Tile-floor rooms range from small, simple studios (some with ocean-view balconies) to two-bedroom suites with peaked ceilings and whirlpool tubs; all have kitchenettes. The restaurant serves good, reasonably priced meals. Use of a bank of Internet-connected computers near the reception area is free. *J. E. Irausquin Blvd. 252, Eagle Beach, tel. 297/587–1492 or 800/932–6509, fax 297/587–1463. www.amsterdammanor.com. 37 rooms, 35 suites. Restaurant, fans, in-room safes, kitchenettes, microwaves, cable TV with movies, pool, wading pool, snorkeling, bar, playground, laundry facilities, Wi-Fi, car rental, some pets allowed.* AE, D, MC, V. EP.

$$ **BOARDWALK VACATION RETREAT.** The owners describe this small hotel as offering "far-from-it-all tranquillity with close-to-it-all convenience." A stay here puts you only a few yards from the

beach and water sports and within walking distance of casinos. Yet, despite its great location, the property manages to remain well insulated from the hustle and bustle. The suites are in *casitas* enveloped by gardens where hummingbirds and butterflies dart among exotic palm trees. The rooms have comfortable rattan furnishings, large living rooms and kitchens, and patios with barbecue grills and hammocks. Housekeeping is provided every other day, and laundry service is available. *Bakval 20, Palm Beach, tel. 297/586–6654, fax 297/586–1836. www.theboardwalk-aruba.com. 13 units. Grocery, kitchenettes, microwaves, refrigerators, cable TV, in-room VCRs, pool, wading pool, hot tub, babysitting. AE, D, MC, V. EP.*

$$ **BRICKELL BAY BEACH CLUB.** Located a few minutes from the high-rise hotels and Palm Beach, Brickell Bay compensates by offering great rates. Rooms are bright with sunny exposures, though there are no ocean views. The pool area is usually lively, as is Tomato Charlie's Pizza—the hotel restaurant. Golf carts ferry guests to the beach and the Excelsior Casino. Nearby are several great restaurants and the SETAR offices, where you can rent a cell phone or buy Wi-Fi access (for a lot less than most hotels charge). *J. E. Irausquin Blvd. 370, Palm Beach, tel. 297/586–0900, fax 297/586–4957. www.brickellbayaruba.com. 94 rooms, 3 suites. Coffee shop, grocery, cable TV, pool, video game room, Internet, meeting rooms, some pets allowed. AE, D, DC, MC, V. EP.*

$$ **CARIBBEAN PALM VILLAGE.** Lush gardens lend an air of tranquillity to this tile-roof resort not far from Palm Beach. Some of the one- and two-bedroom accommodations have fully equipped kitchens; all have private balconies. Eat breakfast or lunch at the pool bar, then swim a few laps or serve up a few aces on the tennis court. The hotel, a short walk from restaurants, casinos, and nightclubs, generally attracts people over 30. Although Eagle Beach is only a 10-minute walk from the resort, free shuttle buses depart for the sand weekdays at 9:25 AM and 2:25 PM and return at 12:30 PM and 4 PM. Valentino's, one of the best restaurants on the island, is in the compound. *Palm Beach Rd., Noord 43E, Noord, tel. 297/586–*

2700, fax 297/586–2380. www.cpvr.com. 170 rooms. Restaurant, fans, kitchens, microwaves, refrigerators, cable TV, tennis court, 2 pools, hot tub, bar, babysitting, car rental. AE, DC, MC, V. EP.

$$ DIVI DUTCH VILLAGE. Enjoy old-world ambience while basking in new-world comforts at this oceanfront time-share set around a pair of free-form freshwater pools. Many handcrafted accents adorn the Spanish-style rooms, which have kitchens and hot tubs. Larger rooms also have private patios or balconies. This is the quietest part of the Divi complex; it attracts a mainly European crowd. The rates are the cheapest of all the Divi properties, and the rooms are generally bigger—but there are no ocean views. You can participate in various outdoor activities and dine in one of several restaurants at the adjoining resorts. Kids under 15 stay free. Guest have access to the facilities of all Divi resorts on Aruba. *J. E. Irausquin Blvd. 47, Oranjestad, tel. 297/583–5000 or 800/367–3484, fax 297/582–0501. www.diviresorts.com. 97 units. Kitchenettes, microwaves, refrigerators, cable TV, golf privileges, 2 pools, hot tubs, beach, Internet, some pets allowed. AE, D, DC, MC, V. EP.*

$$ HOLIDAY INN SUNSPREE ARUBA BEACH RESORT & CASINO. Three seven-story buildings filled with spacious rooms are set along a sugary, palm-dotted shore. The pool's cascades and sundeck draw as large a crowd as the beach, where you can join the Wednesday evening cocktail party. Enjoy live entertainment as you try your luck at the casino. This hotel is exceptionally popular with tour groups, so the reception lines can be a bit daunting at peak times. None of the on-site restaurants are especially memorable, but there are excellent alternatives across the road and at the neighboring resorts. The free program for kids is a boon for families. *J. E. Irausquin Blvd. 230, Palm Beach, tel. 297/586–3600 or 800/934–6750, fax 297/586–5165. www.aruba.sunspreeresorts.com. 600 rooms, 7 suites. 4 restaurants, refrigerators, cable TV with movies, 4 tennis courts, 2 pools, gym, hair salon, massage, beach, dive shop, dock, snorkeling, windsurfing, boating, waterskiing, basketball, Ping-Pong, volleyball, 3 bars, casino, video game room,* *shops, children's programs (ages 5–12), concierge, Internet, meeting rooms. AE, D, DC, MC, V. EP.*

$$ LA QUINTA BEACH RESORT. A relaxed atmosphere makes this time-share resort appealing. One-, two-, and three-bedroom apartments have living-dining areas and kitchenettes. All except the very smallest have balconies with garden or ocean views, and many have their own hot tubs. Daily housekeeping is a real perk. The resort is adjacent to the Alhambra Casino and across the street from the beach. *L. G. Smith Blvd. 228, Eagle Beach, tel. 297/587–5010, fax 297/587–6263. www.webnova.com/laquinta. 54 units. Kitchenettes, microwaves, refrigerators, cable TV, 2 pools, bar, babysitting, laundry service, Internet, car rental. AE, D, MC, V. EP.*

$$ MILL RESORT & SUITES. With clean geometric lines, the architecture of this small resort is striking. Whitewashed, red-roof buildings surround open-air common areas. Rooms are bright and attractive. Junior suites have sitting areas and kitchenettes. Smaller studios have full kitchens, tiny baths, and no balconies. The beach is only a five-minute walk away; free coffee and a weekly scuba lesson are among the on-site amenities. At the Garden Café a special menu offers three courses at affordable prices. Board Fido or Fluffy overnight at the nearby vet. *J. E. Irausquin Blvd. 330, Oranjestad, tel. 297/586–7700, fax 297/586–7271. www.millresort.com. 64 studios, 128 suites. Restaurant, grocery, in-room safes, kitchenettes, microwaves, cable TV, 2 tennis courts, 2 pools, wading pool, gym, massage, sauna, bar, laundry facilities, Internet, car rental, travel services. AE, D, DC, MC, V. EP.*

$–$$ MANCHEBO BEACH RESORT & SPA. Set amid 100 acres of gardens, this resort feels miles away from it all; in reality it's just five minutes from town and across from a complex with shops, restaurants, and a casino. Rooms are decorated with blond-wood furnishings and bright floral fabrics and are equipped with coffeemakers. Guests who choose to purchase the all-inclusive package are treated to à-la-carte breakfast at the poolside Garden Terrace, lunch at the Pega Pega restaurant, dinner at the French

Steakhouse (famous for Argentine-style steaks), and unlimited house drinks at the bar. A pavilion on one of the prettiest stretches of Eagle Beach is the site of many weddings. *J. E. Irausquin Blvd. 55, Eagle Beach, tel. 297/582–3444 or 800/223–1108, fax 297/583–2446. www.manchebo.com. 71 rooms. 2 restaurants, snack bar, fans, in-room safes, refrigerators, cable TV, pool, beach, snorkeling, 2 bars, shops, Internet, car rental. AE, D, DC, MC, V. EP, AI.*

$–$$ TALK OF THE TOWN HOTEL & BEACH CLUB. This property offers excellent rates and a fairly convenient location—it's just a 10-minute walk from downtown. The facilities are built around a courtyard with a large, palm-fringed pool. The hotel underwent a massive renovation and change in management, and all rooms are bright and airy (some include kitchenettes). The Moonlight Patio Bar & Grill restaurant just off the lobby offers reasonably priced meals. Surfside beach is across the road—but be careful as you cross the busy thoroughfare. *L. G. Smith Blvd. 2, Oranjestad, tel. 297/582–3380, fax 297/583–2446. www.tottaruba.com. 63 rooms. Restaurant, in-room safes, kitchenettes, microwaves, refrigerators, cable TV, pool, hot tub, bar, laundry service, meeting rooms. AE, MC, V. EP.*

$–$$ VISTALMAR. Alby and Katy Yarzagary converted this property across the street from the fishing pier into a homey inn. Simply furnished one-bedroom apartments each have a full kitchen, a living-dining area, and a sunny porch. The Yarzagarys provide snorkeling gear and stock arriving guests' refrigerators with breakfast fixings. There's no beach at this spot south of town, but the sea is just across the street. The major drawback is the distance from shopping and dining options, but it's only 5 minutes from the airport. *Bucutiweg 28, Oranjestad, tel. 297/582–8579, fax 297/582–2200. www.arubavistalmar.com. 8 rooms. Kitchenettes, microwaves, cable TV with movies, laundry facilities, car rental. D. CP.*

¢–$ MVC EAGLE BEACH. Located across from Eagle Beach, this former vacation facility for the visiting families of Dutch marines is an excellent bargain. Most guests are budget-minded Dutch tourists, who can live with impeccably clean but basic rooms—don't come expecting the facilities of a Hilton. However, there is a tennis court, a good restaurant serving hearty fare, and a lively bar. Families with small children will appreciate the ample play areas and kiddie pool. *Irausquin Blvd. 240, Eagle Beach, tel. 297/587–0110, fax 297/587–0117. www.mvceaglebeach.com. 16 rooms, 3 suites. Restaurant, tennis court, pool, wading pool, beach, Ping-Pong, bar, playground, laundry facilities; no room TVs. MC, V. EP.*

practical information

There are planners and there are those who, excuse the pun, fly by the seat of their pants. We happily place ourselves among the planners. Our writers and editors try to anticipate all the issues you may face before and during any journey, and then they do their research. This section is the product of their efforts. Use it to get excited about your trip to Aruba, to inform your travel planning, or to guide you on the road should the seat of your pants start to feel threadbare.

Addresses

"Informal" might best describe Aruban addresses. Sometimes the street designation is in English (as in J. E. Irausquin Blvd.), other times in Dutch (as in Wilhelminastraat); sometimes it's not specified whether something is a boulevard or a *straat* (street) at all. Street numbers follow street names, and postal codes aren't used. In rural areas, you might have to ask a local for directions—and be prepared for such instructions as "Take a right at the market, then a left where you see the big divi-divi tree."

Air Travel

There are nonstop flights to Aruba from Charlotte, Chicago (seasonal service), Houston, Miami, Newark, New York–JFK, and Philadelphia. Canadian travelers may fly nonstop during high travel season but must connect through the United States or Caracas, Venezuela, at other times.

BOOKING YOUR FLIGHT

When you book **look for nonstop flights** and **remember that "direct" flights stop at least once.** Try to avoid connecting flights, which require a change of plane. Two airlines may operate a connecting flight jointly, so ask if your airline operates every segment of the trip; you may find that the carrier you prefer flies you only part of the way. To find more booking tips and to check prices and make online flight reservations, log on to www.fodors.com.

CARRIERS

American Airlines offers daily nonstop service from Miami, New York, and San Juan, and weekly service from Boston; American Eagle also flies from San Juan daily. Continental Airlines has nonstop service daily from Houston and Newark. Delta flies nonstop daily from Atlanta and weekly from New York–JFK. KLM offers regular service from Amsterdam. United flies weekly from Chicago and seasonally from Dulles in Washington, D.C. US Airways flies daily from Charlotte and Philadelphia. Air Canada offers weekly nonstop flights from Toronto during high travel season (November–April). At press time, JetBlue was set to begin daily nonstop service between New York–JFK and Aruba on September 15, 2006.

BonairExpress offers connecting flights to Bonaire, Curaçao, and St. Maarten.

Check with the airlines during high travel season for flight and route additions, as service is sometimes increased in response to a rise in tourism.

➤**AIRLINES & CONTACTS: AIR CANADA** (tel. 297/582–6401 on Aruba, 888/247–2262 in North America, www.aircanada.com). **American/American Eagle** (tel. 297/582–2700 on Aruba, 800/433–7300 in North America, www.aa.com). **BonairExpress** (tel. 599/717–0808, www.bonairexpress.com). **Continental** (tel. 297/588–0044 on Aruba, 800/231–0856 in North America, www.continental.com). **Delta** (tel. 297/588–0044 on Aruba, 800/241–

4141 in North America, www.delta.com). **JetBlue** (tel. 800/538-2583, www.jetblue.com). **KLM** (tel. 297/582–3546 on Aruba, 31/20–4–747–747 in Amsterdam, www.klm.com in the Netherlands). **United Airlines** (tel. 297/588–6544 on Aruba, 800/538–2929 in North America, www.united.com). **US Airways** (tel. 297/800–1580 on Aruba, 800/622–1015 in North America, www.usairways.com).

➤**AIRLINE COMPLAINTS: Office of Aviation Enforcement and Proceedings** (Aviation Consumer Protection Division) (tel. 202/366–2220, airconsumer.ost.dot.gov). **Federal Aviation Administration Consumer Hotline** (tel. 866/835–5322, www.faa.gov).

CHECK-IN & BOARDING

Checking in, paying departure taxes (if they aren't included in your ticket), clearing security, and boarding can take time on Aruba. Because security has gotten tighter, **get to the airport at least three hours ahead of time.** You may be randomly selected for inspection of your carry-on baggage at the gate. Regulations prohibit packing certain items in your carry-on luggage, including matches, lighters, and handheld radios. Check with your hotel concierge before packing to return home.

Double-check your flight times, especially if you made your reservations far in advance. Airlines change their schedules, and alerts may not reach you. Always **bring a government-issued photo I.D. to the airport;** even when it's not required, a passport is best (starting December 31, 2006, a passport will be required to enter or reenter the United States from the Caribbean). **Arrive when you need to and not before.** Check-in is usually at least two to three hours before international flights, but many airlines have more stringent advance check-in requirements at some busy airports. The TSA estimates the waiting time for security at most major airports and publishes the information on its Web site. Note that if you aren't at the gate at least

10 minutes before your flight is scheduled to take off (sometimes earlier), you won't be allowed to board.

Don't stand in a line if you don't have to. Buy an e-ticket, check in at an electronic kiosk, or—even better—check in on your airline's Web site before you leave home. If you don't need to check luggage, you could bypass all but the security lines. These days, most domestic airline tickets are electronic; international tickets may be either electronic or paper.

You usually pay a surcharge (up to $50) to get a paper ticket, and its sole advantage is that it may be easier to endorse over to another airline if your flight is cancelled and the airline with which you booked can't accommodate you on another flight. With an e-ticket, the only thing you receive is an e-mailed receipt citing your itinerary and reservation and ticket numbers. Be sure to carry this with you as you'll need it to get past security. If you lose you receipt, though, you can simply print out another copy or ask the airline to do it for you at check-in.

Particularly during busy travel seasons and around holiday periods, if a flight is oversold, the gate agent will usually ask for volunteers and will offer some sort of compensation if you are willing to take a different flight. **Know your rights.** If you are bumped from a flight *involuntarily*, the airline must give you some kind of compensation if an alternate flight can't be found within one hour. If your flight is delayed because of something within the airline's control (so bad weather doesn't count), then the airline has a responsibility to get you to your destination on the same day, even if they have to book you on another airline and in an upgraded class if necessary. Read your airline's Contract of Carriage; it's usually buried somewhere on the airline's Web site.

Be prepared to quickly adjust your plans by programming a few numbers into your cell: your airline, an airport hotel or two, your destination hotel, your car service, and/or your travel agent.

Bring snacks, water, and sufficient diversions, and you'll be covered if you get stuck in the airport, on the Tarmac, or even in the air during turbulence.

FLYING TIMES

Aruba is 2½ hours from Miami, 4½ hours from New York, and 9½ hours from Amsterdam. The flight from New York to San Juan, Puerto Rico, takes 3½ hours; from Miami to San Juan it's 1½ hours; and from San Juan to Aruba it's just over an hour. Shorter still is the ¼- to ½-hour hop (depending on whether you take a prop or a jet plane) from Curaçao to Aruba.

Airport & Transfers

AIRPORT

Aruba's Aeropuerto Internacional Reina Beatrix (Queen Beatrix International Airport), near the island's south coast, is a modern, passenger-friendly facility. Renovations in 2001 brought new concession areas, business lounges, escalators, elevators, restrooms, covered walkways, and baggage-claim areas.

➤**AIRPORT INFORMATION: Aeropuerto Internacional Reina Beatrix** (tel. 297/582–4800, www.airportaruba.com).

TRANSFERS

A taxi from the airport to most hotels takes about 20 minutes. It will cost about $16 to get to the hotels along Eagle Beach, $18 to the high-rise hotels on Palm Beach, and $9 to the hotels downtown. You'll find a taxi stand right outside the baggage-claim area.

Business Hours

Bank hours are weekdays 8:15 to 5:45, with some branches closing for lunch from noon to 1. The Caribbean Mercantile Bank at the airport is open Saturday 9 to 4 and Sunday 9 to 1. The central post office in Oranjestad, catercorner from the San

Francisco Church, is open weekdays 7:30 to noon and 1 to 4:30. Shops are generally open Monday through Saturday 8:30 to 6. Some stores close for lunch from noon to 2. Many shops also open when cruise ships are in port on Sunday and holidays.

Bus Travel

Each day, from 6 AM to midnight, buses make hourly trips between the beach hotels and downtown Oranjestad. The one-way fare is $1.25, and the round-trip fare is $2. Exact change is preferred. Buses also run down the coast from Oranjestad to San Nicolas for the same fare. Contact the Aruba Tourism Authority for schedules. Buses run from the airport terminal to hotels every 15 minutes during the day until 8 PM, and once an hour from 8:40 PM to 12:40 AM.

Car Rental

Your driver's license may not be recognized outside your home country. You may not be able to rent a car without an International driving permit (IDP), which can be used only in conjunction with a valid driver's license and which translates your license into 10 languages. Check the AAA Web site for more info as well as for IDPs ($10) themselves.

You must meet the minimum age requirements of each rental service (Budget, for example, requires drivers to be over 25; Avis, over 23; and Hertz, over 21). A signed credit-card slip or a cash deposit of $500 is required. Rates for unlimited mileage are between $35 and $65 a day, with local agencies generally offering lower rates. Insurance is available starting at about $10 per day. Try to make reservations before arriving, and opt for a four-wheel-drive vehicle if you plan to explore the island.

➤**Agencies: Avis** (Kolibristraat 14, Oranjestad, tel. 297/582–8787 or 800/522–9696, www.avis.com; Airport, tel. 297/582–5496). **Budget** (Kolibristraat 1, Oranjestad, tel. 297/582–8600 or 800/472–3325, www.budget.com). **Economy** (Kolibristraat 5, tel. 297/582–5176, www.economyaruba.com). **Hedwina Car Rental** (Bubali 93A, Noord, tel. 297/587–6442; Airport, tel. 297/583–0880). **Hertz** (Sabana Blanco 35, near the airport, tel. 297/582–1845 or 800/654–3001, www.hertz.com; Airport, tel. 297/582–9112). **National** (Tanki Leendert 170, Noord, tel. 297/587–1967 or 800/227–7368, www.nationalcar.com; Airport, tel. 297/582–5451). **Thrifty** (Balashi 65, Santa Cruz, tel. 297/585–5300, www.thrifty.com; Airport, tel. 297/583–5335).

INSURANCE

Everyone who rents a car wonders about whether the insurance that the rental companies offer is worth the expense. No one—not even us—has a simple answer. This is particularly true abroad, where laws are different than at home.

If you own a car, your personal auto insurance may cover a rental to some degree, though not all policies protect you abroad; always read your policy's fine print. If you don't have auto insurance, then seriously consider buying the collision- or loss-damage waiver (CDW or LDW) from the car-rental company, which eliminates your liability for damage to the car. Some credit cards offer CDW coverage, but it's usually supplemental to your own insurance and rarely covers SUVs, minivans, luxury models, and the like. If your coverage is secondary, you may still be liable for loss-of-use costs from the car-rental company. But no credit-card insurance is valid unless you use that card for *all* transactions, from reserving to paying the final bill. All companies exclude car rental in some countries, so be sure to find out about the destination to which you are traveling.

Some countries require you to purchase CDW coverage or require car-rental companies to include it in quoted rates. Ask your rental company about issues like these in your destination. In most cases, it's cheaper to add a supplemental CDW plan to your comprehensive travel insurance policy than to purchase it from a rental company. That said, you don't want to pay for a supplement if you're required to buy insurance from the rental company.

Note that you can decline the insurance from the rental company and purchase it through a third-party provider such as Travel Guard (www.travelguard.com)—$9 per day for $35,000 of coverage. That's sometimes just under half the price of the CDW offered by some car-rental companies. Also, Diners Club offers primary CDW coverage on all rentals reserved and paid for with the card. This means that Diners Club's company—not your own car insurance—pays in case of an accident. It *doesn't* mean your car-insurance company won't raise your rates once it discovers you had an accident.

Car Travel

Most of Aruba's major attractions are fairly easy to find; others you'll happen upon only by sheer luck (or with an Aruban friend). Aside from the major highways, the island's winding roads are poorly marked (although the situation is slowly improving). International traffic signs and Dutch-style traffic signals (with an extra light for a turning lane) can be misleading if you're not used to them; use extreme caution, especially at intersections, until you grasp the rules of the road. Speed limits are rarely posted but are usually 80 kph (50 mph) in the countryside.

GASOLINE

Gas prices average a little more than $1 a liter (roughly ¼ gallon), which is reasonable by Caribbean standards. Stations are plentiful in and near Oranjestad, San Nicolas, and Santa Cruz and near the major high-rise hotels on the western coast. All take cash, and most take major credit cards.

PARKING

There aren't any parking meters in downtown Oranjestad, and finding an open spot is very difficult. Try the lot on Calle G. F.

Betico Croes across from the First National Bank, the one on Havenstraat near the Chez Matilde restaurant, or the one on Emanstraat near the water tower. Rates average $1.25 an hour, but some charge almost twice that.

Children on Aruba

If your kids love the beach, they'll love Aruba. Resorts are increasingly sensitive to families' needs, and many now have playgrounds and extensive children's programs, and can arrange for babysitters.

FLYING

If your children are two or older, **ask about children's airfares.** As a general rule, infants under two not occupying a seat fly at greatly reduced fares or even for free. But if you want to guarantee a seat for an infant, you have to pay full fare. Consider flying during off-peak days and times; most airlines will grant an infant a seat without a ticket if there are available seats.When booking, **confirm carry-on allowances** if you're traveling with infants. In general, for babies charged 10% to 50% of the adult fare you are allowed one carry-on bag and a collapsible stroller; if the flight is full, the stroller may have to be checked or you may be limited to less.

Experts agree that it's a good idea to use safety seats aloft for children weighing less than 40 pounds. Airlines set their own policies: if you use a safety seat, U.S. carriers usually require that the child be ticketed, even if he or she is young enough to ride free, because the seats must be strapped into regular seats. And even if you pay the full adult fare for the seat, it may be worth it, especially on longer trips. Do **check your airline's policy about using safety seats during takeoff and landing.** Safety seats are not allowed everywhere in the plane, so get your seat assignments as early as possible.

When reserving, request children's meals or a freestanding bassinet (not available on all airlines) if you need them. But note that bulkhead seats, where you must sit to use the bassinet, may lack an overhead bin or storage space on the floor.

FOOD

Even if your youngsters are picky eaters, meals in the Caribbean shouldn't be a problem. Baby food is easy to find, and hamburgers and hot dogs are available at many resorts. Restaurant menus offer pasta, pizza, sandwiches, and ice cream. Supermarkets have cereal, snacks, and other packaged goods you'll recognize from home.

LODGING

Children are welcome in most Aruban resorts, and those under 12 or 16 can often stay free in their parents' room. Be sure to **find out the cutoff age for children's discounts** when booking.

PRECAUTIONS

To avoid immigration problems if your child has a different last name, **bring identification that clarifies the family relationship** (e.g., a birth certificate identifying the parent or a joint passport).

SUPPLIES & EQUIPMENT

Suites at many resorts and even small hotels have sofa beds suitable for children sharing a parent's room. High chairs and cribs are also generally available. Supermarkets sell common brands of disposable diapers, baby food, and other necessities. Bookstores and souvenir shops have activity books and toys that kids will enjoy on vacation and back at home.

Cruise Travel

Cruising is a relaxed and convenient way to tour this beautiful part of the world: you get all of the amenities of a luxury hotel and enough activities to guarantee fun, even on rainy days. All your important decisions are made long before you board. Your itinerary is set, and you know the total cost of your vacation beforehand.

Ships usually call at several ports on a single voyage but are at each for only one day. To learn how to plan, choose, and book a cruise-ship voyage, consult *Fodor's Complete Guide to Caribbean Cruises* (available in bookstores everywhere).

➤**CRUISE LINES: Carnival Cruise Line** (tel. 305/599–2600 or 800/227–6482, www.carnival.com). **Celebrity Cruises** (tel. 305/539–6000 or 800/437–3111, www.celebrity.com). **Crystal Cruises** (tel. 310/785–9300 or 800/446–6620, www.crystalcruises.com). **Cunard Line** (tel. 661/753–1000 or 800/728–6273, www.cunard.com). **Holland America Line** (tel. 206/281-3535 or 877/932-4259, www.hollandamerica.com). **Norwegian Cruise Line** (tel. 305/436–4000 or 800/327–7030, www.ncl.com). **Princess Cruises** (tel. 661/753–0000 or 800/774–6237, www.princess.com). **Regent Seven Seas Cruises** (tel. 954/776–6123 or 800/477–7500, www.rssc.com). **Royal Caribbean International** (tel. 305/539–6000 or 800/327–6700, www.royalcaribbean.com). **Seabourn Cruise Line** (tel. 305/463–3000 or 800/929–9391, www.seabourn.com). **Star Clippers** (tel. 305/442–0550 or 800/442–0551, www.starclippers.com). **Windstar Cruises** (tel. 206/281–3535 or 800/258–7245, www.windstarcruises.com).

➤**ORGANIZATIONS: Cruise Lines International Association** (CLIA) (tel. 212/921–0066, www.cruising.org).

Customs & Duties

IN ARUBA

You can bring up to 1 liter of spirits, 3 liters of beer, or 2.25 liters of wine per person, and up to 200 cigarettes or 50 cigars into Aruba. You don't need to declare the value of gifts or other items, although customs officials may inquire about large items or large quantities of items and charge (at their discretion) an import tax of 7.5% to 22% on items worth more than $230. Meat, birds, and illegal substances are forbidden. You may be asked to provide written verification that plants are free of diseases. If you're traveling with pets, bring a veterinarian's note attesting to their good health.

➤**ARUBA CUSTOMS OFFICE:** (tel. 297/582–1800).

IN THE U.S.

You're always allowed to bring goods of a certain value back home without having to pay any duty or import tax. There's also a limit on the amount of tobacco and liquor you can bring back duty-free, and some countries have separate limits for perfumes; for exact figures, check with your customs department. The values of so-called "duty-free" goods are included in these amounts. When you shop abroad, save all your receipts as customs inspectors may ask to see them as well as the items you purchased. If the total value of your goods is more than the duty-free limit, then you'll have to pay a tax (most often a flat percentage) on the value of everything beyond that limit.

➤**U.S. CUSTOMS AND BORDER PROTECTION:** (www.cbp.gov).

Electricity

Aruba runs on a 110-volt cycle, the same as in the United States; outlets are usually the two-prong variety. Total blackouts are rare, and most large hotels have backup generators.

Emergencies

➤**CONTACTS: Air Ambulance** (tel. 297/582–9197). **Ambulance and Fire** (tel. 911). **Botica Eagle Pharmacy** (L. G. Smith Blvd., near hospital, tel. 297/587–6103). **Horacio Oduber Hospital** (L. G. Smith Blvd., across from Costa Linda Beach Resort and the Alhambra Casino, tel. 297/587–4300). **Police** (tel. 911).

Etiquette & Behavior

It's best not to mention to residents how "American" everything is—many have settled here from South America and Europe. Aruba has a separate status with the Kingdom of the Netherlands, allowing it to handle its own aviation, customs, immigration, communications, and other internal matters, but the island does retain strong economic, cultural, and political ties with Holland.

Health

DIVERS' ALERT

Don't fly within 24 hours of scuba diving. In an emergency, Air Ambulance, run by Richard Rupert, will fly you to Curaçao at a low altitude if you need to get to a decompression chamber.

FOOD & DRINK

As a rule, water is pure and food is wholesome in hotels and local restaurants throughout Aruba, but **be cautious when buying food from street vendors.** And just as you would at home, **wash or peel all fruits and vegetables** before eating them. Traveler's diarrhea, caused by consuming contaminated water, unpasteurized milk and milk products, and unrefrigerated food, isn't a big problem—unless it happens to you. So **watch what you eat,** especially at outdoor buffets in the hot sun. Make sure cooked food is hot and cold food has been properly refrigerated.

Mild cases of diarrhea may respond to Imodium (known generically as loperamide) or Pepto-Bismol (not as strong), both of which can be purchased in local pharmacies. Drink plenty of bottled water to keep from becoming dehydrated. A salt-sugar solution (½ teaspoon salt and 4 tablespoons sugar per quart of water) is a good remedy for rehydrating yourself.

PESTS & OTHER HAZARDS

The major health risk is sunburn or sunstroke. A long-sleeve shirt, a hat, and long pants or a beach wrap are essential on a boat, for midday at the beach, and whenever you go out sightseeing. **Use sunscreen** with an SPF of at least 15—especially if you're fair—and apply it liberally on your nose, ears, and other sensitive and exposed areas. Make sure the sunscreen is waterproof if you're engaging in water sports. Always **limit your sun time** for the first few days and **drink plenty of liquids.** Limit intake of caffeine and alcohol, which hasten dehydration.

Mosquitoes and flies can be bothersome, so **pack strong repellent** (the ones that contain DEET or Picaridin are the most effective). The strong trade winds are a relief in the subtropical climate, but don't hang your bathing suit on a balcony—it will probably blow away. Help Arubans conserve water and energy: turn off air-conditioning when you leave your room, and don't let water run unattended.

SHOTS & MEDICATIONS

No special shots or vaccinations are required for Caribbean destinations.

➤**HEALTH WARNINGS: National Centers for Disease Control & Prevention** (CDC) (tel. 877/394–8747 international travelers' health line, www.cdc.gov/travel). **World Health Organization** (WHO) www.who.int).

Holidays

Aruba's official holidays are New Year's Day, Good Friday, Easter Sunday, and Christmas, as well as Betico Croes Day (January 25), National Anthem and Flag Day (March 18), Queen's Day

(April 30), Labor Day (May 1), and Ascension Day (May 17 in 2007, May 1 in 2008, May 21 in 2009).

Lodging

Assume that hotels operate on the **European Plan** (EP, with no meals) unless we specify that they use the **Continental Plan** (CP, with a continental breakfast), **Modified American Plan** (MAP, with breakfast and dinner), or are **All-Inclusive** (AI).

Mail & Shipping

From Aruba to the United States or Canada, a letter costs Afl1.40 (about 80¢) and a postcard costs Afl.60 (35¢). Expect it to take one to two weeks. When addressing letters to Aruba, don't worry about the lack of formal addresses or postal codes; the island's postal service knows where to go.

If you need to send a package in a hurry, there are a few options to get the job done. The Federal Express office across from the airport offers overnight service to the United States if you get your package in before 3 PM. Another big courier service is UPS, and there are also several smaller local courier services that provide international deliveries, most of them open weekdays 9 to 5. Check the local phone book for details.

➤**COURIER SERVICES: Federal Express** (Browninvest Financial Center, Wayaca 31-A, Oranjestad, tel. 297/592–9039). **UPS** (Rockefellerstraat 3, Oranjestad, tel. 297/582–8646).

Money Matters

CURRENCY

Arubans happily accept U.S. dollars virtually everywhere. That said, there's no real need to exchange money, except for necessary pocket change (for soda machines or pay phones). The official currency is the Aruban florin (Afl), also called the guilder, which is made up of 100 cents. Silver coins come in denominations of 1, 2½, 5, 10, 25, and 50 (the square one) cents. Paper currency comes in denominations of 5, 10, 25, 50, and 100 florins.

At press time exchange rates were Afl1.79 per U.S. dollar and Afl1.58 per Canadian dollar. Stores, hotels, and restaurants converted at Afl1.80; supermarkets and gas stations at Afl1.75. The Dutch Antillean florin—used on Bonaire and Curaçao—isn't accepted here. Prices quoted throughout this book are in U.S. dollars unless otherwise noted.

ATMS

If you need fast cash, you'll find ATMs that accept international cards (and dispense cash in the local currency) at banks in Oranjestad, at the major malls, and along the roads leading to the hotel strip.

➤**BANKS: RBTT Bank** (Caya G. F. Betico Croes 89, Oranjestad, tel. 297/582–1515). **Caribbean Mercantile Bank** (Caya G. F. Betico Croes 5, Oranjestad, tel. 297/582–3118).

CREDIT CARDS & TRAVELER'S CHECKS

Major credit cards are widely accepted at hotels, restaurants, shops, car-rental agencies, and other service providers throughout Aruba. The only places that might not accept them are open-air markets or tiny shops in out-of-the way villages.

It's smart to **write down the account numbers of the credit cards you're carrying** and the toll-free numbers to call in case your cards are lost or stolen.

Throughout this guide the following abbreviations are used: **AE,** American Express; **D,** Discover; **DC,** Diners Club; **MC,** MasterCard; and **V,** Visa.

SERVICE CHARGES, TIPPING & TAXES

Hotels usually add an 11% service charge to the bill and collect 8% in government taxes for a whopping total of 19% on top of quoted rates. Restaurants generally include a 10%–15% service charge on the bill; when in doubt, ask. If service isn't included, a 10% tip is standard; if it is included, it's still customary to add something extra, usually small change, at your discretion. Taxi drivers expect a 10%–15% tip, but it isn't mandatory. Porters and bellhops should receive about $2 per bag; chambermaids about $2 a day, but check to see if their tips are included in your bill so you don't overpay. The airport departure tax is $36.75 for flights to the United States and $33.50 to other destinations, but the fee is usually included in your ticket price. Children under two don't pay departure tax. For purchases you'll pay a 6.5% ABB tax (a value-added tax) in all but the duty-free shops.

TRAVELER'S CHECKS

Get traveler's checks in small denominations—$20 or $50. Restaurants and most shops will accept them (with I.D.), and your hotel will cash them for you, though you might get change in local currency. In rural areas and small villages you'll need cash. Lost or stolen checks can usually be replaced within 24 hours. **Buy and pay for your own traveler's checks;** the person who bought the checks must request the refund.

Packing

Why do some people travel with a convoy of suitcases the size of large-screen TVs and yet never have a thing to wear? How do others pack a toaster-oven-size duffle with a week's worth of outfits *and* supplies for every possible contingency? We realize that packing is a matter of style—a very personal thing—but there's a lot to be said for traveling light. The tips in this section will help you win the battle of the bulging bag.

Make a list. In a recent Fodor's survey, 29% of respondents said they make lists (and often pack) at least a week before a trip. Lists can be used at least twice—once to pack and once to repack at the end of your trip. You'll also have a record of the contents of your suitcase, just in case it disappears in transit.

Think it through. What's the weather like? Is this a business trip or a cruise or resort vacation? Going abroad? In some places and/or sights, traditions of dress may be more or less conservative than you're used to. As your itinerary comes together, jot activities down and note possible outfits next to each (don't forget those shoes and accessories).

Edit your wardrobe. Plan to wear everything twice (better yet, thrice) and to do laundry along the way. Stick to one basic look—urban chic, sporty casual, etc. Build around one or two neutrals and an accent (e.g., black, white, and olive green). Women can freshen looks by changing scarves or jewelry. For a week's trip, you can look smashing with three bottoms, four or five tops, a sweater, and a jacket you can wear alone or over the sweater.

Be practical. Put comfortable shoes at the top of your list. (Did we need to tell you this?) Pack items that are lightweight, wrinkle resistant, compact, and washable. (Or this?) Try a simple wrinkling test: Intentionally fold a piece of fabric between your fingers for a couple minutes. If it refuses to crease, it will probably come out of your suitcase looking fresh. That said if you stack and then roll your clothes when packing, they'll wrinkle less.

Check weight and size limitations. In the United States you may be charged extra for checked bags weighing more than 50 pounds. Abroad some airlines don't allow you to check bags weighing more than 60 to 70 pounds, or they charge outrageous fees for every pound your luggage is over. Carry-on size limitations can be stringent, too.

Be prepared to lug it yourself. If there's one thing that can turn a pack rat into a minimalist, it's a vacation spent lugging heavy bags over long distances. Unless you're on a guided tour or a cruise, select luggage that you can readily carry. Porters, like good butlers, are hard to find these days.

Lock it up. Several companies sell locks (about $10) approved by the Transportation Safety Administration that can be unlocked by all U.S. security personnel should they decide to search your bags. Alternatively, you can use simple plastic cable ties, which are sold at hardware stores in bundles.

Tag it. Always put tags on your luggage with some kind of contact information; use your business address if you don't want people to know your home address. Put the same information (and a copy of your itinerary) inside your luggage, too.

Don't check valuables. On U.S. flights, airlines are only liable for about $2,800 per person for bags. On international flights, the liability limit is around $635 per bag. But just try collecting from the airline for items like computers, cameras, and jewelry. It isn't going to happen; they aren't covered. And though comprehensive travel policies may cover luggage, the liability limit is often a pittance. Your homeowners' policy may cover you sufficiently when you travel—or not. You're really better off stashing baubles and gizmos in your carryon—right near those prescription meds.

Report problems immediately. If your bags—or things in them—are damaged or go astray, file a written claim with your airline *before you leave the airport*. If the airline is at fault, it may give you money for essentials until your luggage arrives. Most lost bags are found within 48 hours, so alert the airline to your whereabouts for two or three days. If your bag was opened for security reasons in the United States and something is missing, file a claim with the TSA.

WHAT TO BRING

Dress on Aruba is generally casual. **Bring loose-fitting clothing made of natural fabrics** to see you through days of heat and humidity. **Pack a beach cover-up,** both to protect yourself from the sun and to provide something to wear to and from your hotel room. Bathing suits and immodest attire are frowned upon away from the beach. A sun hat is advisable, but you don't have to pack one—inexpensive straw hats are available everywhere. For shopping and sightseeing, bring walking shorts, jeans, T-shirts, long-sleeve cotton shirts, slacks, and sundresses. Nighttime dress can range from very informal to casually elegant, depending on the establishment. A tie is practically never required, but a jacket may be appropriate in fancy restaurants. You may need a light sweater or jacket for evenings.

In your carry-on luggage, **pack an extra pair of eyeglasses or contact lenses** (but if you forget, there are several eye-care centers in town where you can pick up a spare pair of lenses) and **enough of any medication you take** to last the entire trip. You may also ask your doctor to write a spare prescription using the drug's generic name, since brand names may vary from country to country. In luggage to be checked, **never pack prescription drugs or valuables.** To avoid customs delays, carry medications in their original packaging. And don't forget to carry with you the addresses of offices that handle refunds of lost traveler's checks.

Passports

Starting December 31, 2006, a passport will be required to enter or reenter the United States from the Caribbean.

We're always surprised at how few Americans have passports—only 25% at this writing. This number is expected to grow in coming years, when it becomes impossible to reenter the United States from trips to neighboring Canada or Mexico without one. Remember this: A passport verifies both your identity and nationality—a great reason to have one.

U.S. passports are valid for 10 years. You must apply in person if you're getting a passport for the first time; if your previous passport was lost, stolen or damaged; or if your previous passport has expired and was issued more than 15 years ago or when you were under 16. All children under 18 must appear in person to apply for or renew a passport. Both parents must accompany any child under 14 (or send a notarized statement with their permission) and provide proof of their relationship to the child.

There are 13 regional passport offices, as well as 7,000 passport acceptance facilities in post offices, public libraries, and other governmental offices. If you're renewing a passport, you can do so by mail. Forms are available at passport acceptance facilities and online.

The cost to apply for a new passport is $97 for adults, $82 for children under 16; renewals are $67. Allow six weeks to process the paperwork for either a new or renewed passport. For an expediting fee of $60, you can reduce the time to about two weeks. If your trip is less than two weeks away, you can get a passport even more rapidly by going to a passport office with the necessary documentation. Private expediters can get things done in as little as 48 hours but charge hefty fees for their services.

Before your trip, make two copies of your passport's data page (one for someone at home and another for you to carry separately). Or scan the page and e-mail it to someone at home and/or yourself.

➤**U.S. PASSPORT INFORMATION: U.S. Department of State** (tel. 877/487–2778, http://travel.state.gov/passport)

➤**U.S. PASSPORT & VISA EXPEDITERS: A. Briggs Passport & Visa Expeditors** (tel. 800/806–0581 or 202/464–3000, www.abriggs.com). **American Passport Express** (tel. 800/455–5166 or 603/559–9888, www.americanpassport.com). **Passport Express** (tel. 800/362–8196 or 401/272–4612, www.passportexpress.com). **Travel Document Systems** (tel. 800/874–5100 or 202/638–3800, www.traveldocs.com). **Travel the World Visas** (tel. 866/886–8472 or 301/495–7700, www.world-visa.com).

Restrooms

Outside of Oranjestad, the only public restrooms you'll find will be in the few restaurants that dot the countryside.

Safety

Arubans are very friendly, so you needn't be afraid to stop and ask anyone for directions. It's a relatively safe island, but commonsense rules still apply. Lock your rental car when you leave it, and leave valuables in your hotel safe. Don't leave bags unattended in the airport, on the beach, or on tour vehicles.

Shopping

For many, shopping on Aruba means duty-free bargains on jewelry, designer clothing, china, crystal, and other luxury goods from around the world. For others, shopping means buying locally produced crafts and works of art.

Bargaining isn't expected in shops, but at open-air markets and with street vendors it may be acceptable. Keep in mind, however, that selling handicrafts or homegrown produce may be a local's only livelihood. When bargaining, consider the amount of work or effort involved and the item's value to you. Vendors don't set artificially high prices and then expect to bargain; they bargain so you'll buy from them instead of their neighbor.

Taxis

There's a dispatch office at the airport; you can also flag down taxis on the street (look for license plates with a "TX" tag). Rates are fixed (i.e., there are no meters; the rates are set by the government and displayed on a chart), though you and the driver should agree on the fare before your ride begins. Add $1 to the fare after midnight and $1 to $3 on Sunday and holidays. An hourlong island tour costs about $30, with up to four people.

Rides into town from Eagle Beach run about $5; from Palm Beach, about $8.

➤**TAXI SERVICE: Airport Taxi Dispatch** (tel. 297/582–2116).

Telephones

To call Aruba direct from the United States, dial 011–297, followed by the seven-digit number in Aruba. (To call from elsewhere abroad, substitute the country of origin's international access code for the 011.) International, direct, and operator-assisted calls from Aruba to all countries in the world are possible via hotel operators or from the Government Long Distance Telephone, Telegraph, and Radio Office (SETAR), in the post-office building in Oranjestad. When making calls on Aruba, simply dial the seven-digit number. AT&T customers can dial 800–8000 from special phones at the cruise dock and in the airport's arrival and departure halls. From other phones dial 121 to contact the SETAR international operator to place a collect or AT&T calling-card call. Local calls from pay phones, which accept both local currency and phone cards, cost 25¢. Business travelers or vacationers who need to be in regular contact with their families at home can rent an international cell phone from the concierge in most hotels or at some local electronics stores.

Tours & Packages

GUIDED TOURS

Guided tours are a good option when you don't want to do it all yourself. You travel along with a group (sometimes large, sometimes small), stay in prebooked hotels, eat with your fellow travelers (sometimes included in the price of your tour, sometimes not), and follow a schedule. A knowledgeable guide can take you places that you might never discover on your own, and you may be pushed to see more than you would have otherwise. Tours aren't for everyone, but they can be just the thing for trips to places where making travel arrangements is difficult or time-consuming (particularly when you don't speak the language). Whenever you book a guided tour, find out what's included and what isn't. A "land-only" tour includes all your travel (by bus, in most cases) in the destination, but not necessarily your flights to or even within it. Also, in most cases, prices in tour brochures don't include fees and taxes. And remember that you'll be expected to tip your guide (in cash) at the end of the tour.

➤**TOUR-OPERATOR RECOMMENDATIONS: American Society of Travel Agents** (ASTA) (tel. 703/739–2782 or 800/965–2782 24-hr hotline, www.astanet.com). **United States Tour Operators Association** (USTOA) (tel. 212/599–6599, www.ustoa.com).

ISLAND TOURS

If you try a cruise around the island, know that the choppy waters are stirred up by trade winds and that catamarans are much smoother than single-hulled boats. Sucking on a peppermint or lemon candy may help a queasy stomach; avoid boating with an empty or overly full stomach. Moonlight cruises cost about $25 per person. There are also snorkeling, dinner and dancing, and sunset party cruises to choose from, priced from $25 to $60 per person. Many of the smaller operators work out of their homes; they often offer to pick you up (and drop you off) at your hotel or meet you at a particular hotel pier.

Explore an underwater reef teeming with marine life without getting wet. Atlantis Submarines operates a 65-foot air-conditioned sub that takes 48 passengers 95–150 feet below the surface along Barcadera Reef. The two-hour trip (including boat transfer to the submarine platform and 50-minute plunge) costs $74. Make reservations one day in advance. Another option is the *Seaworld Explorer*, a semisubmersible that allows you to view Aruba's marine habitat from 6 feet below the surface. The cost is $35 for a 1½-hour tour.

You can see the main sights in one day, but set aside two days to really meander. Guided tours are your best option if you have only a short time. Aruba's Transfer Tour & Taxi C.A. takes you to the main sights on personalized tours that cost $30 per hour.

De Palm Tours has a near monopoly on Aruban sightseeing; you can make reservations through its general office or at hotel tour-desk branches. The company's basic 3½-hour tour hits the highlights. Wear tennis or hiking shoes, and bring a lightweight jacket or wrap (the air-conditioned bus gets cold). It begins at 9:30 AM, picks you up in your hotel lobby, and costs $22.50 per person. A full-day Jeep Adventure tour ($59.50 per person) takes you to sights that would be difficult for you to find on your own. Bring a bandanna to cover your mouth; the ride on rocky dirt roads can get dusty. De Palm also offers full-day tours of Curaçao ($219; every Friday). Prices include round-trip airfare, transfers, sightseeing, and lunch; there's free time for shopping.

Romantic horse-drawn-carriage rides through the city streets of Oranjestad run $30 for a 30-minute tour; hours of operation are 7 PM to 11 PM, and carriages depart from the clock tower at the Royal Plaza Mall.

➤**BOAT TOUR OPERATORS: Atlantis Submarines** (Seaport Village Marina, tel. 297/583–6090). **De Palm Tours** (L. G. Smith Blvd. 142, Oranjestad, tel. 297/582–4400 or 800/766–6016, www.depalm.com). **Pelican Tours & Watersports** (J. E. Irausquin Blvd. 232, Oranjestad, tel. 297/587–2302, www.pelican-aruba.com). **Red Sail Sports** (Seaport Village Mall, L. G. Smith Blvd. 82, Oranjestad, tel. 297/586–1603, 877/733–7245 in the U.S., www.aruba-redsail.com). **Seaworld Explorer** (tel. 297/586–2416).

➤**ORIENTATION TOUR OPERATORS: Aruba's Transfer Tour & Taxi** (Pos Abao 41, Oranjestad, tel. 297/582–2116). **De Palm Tours** (L. G. Smith Blvd. 142, Oranjestad, tel. 297/582–4400 or 800/766–6016, www.depalm.com).

VACATION PACKAGES

Packages *are not* guided tours. Packages combine airfare, accommodations, and perhaps a rental car or other extras (theater tickets, guided excursions, boat trips, reserved entry to popular museums, transit passes), but they let you do your own thing. During busy periods, packages may be your only option because flights and rooms may be otherwise sold out. Packages will definitely save you time. They can also save you money, particularly in peak seasons, but—and this is a really big "but"—you should price each part of the package separately to be sure. And be aware that prices advertised on Web sites and in newspapers rarely include service charges or taxes, which can up your costs by hundreds of dollars.

Note that local tourism boards can provide information about lesser-known and small-niche operators that sell packages to just a few destinations. And don't always assume that you can get the best deal by booking everything yourself. Some packages and cruises are sold only through travel agents.

Each year consumers are stranded or lose their money when packagers—even large ones with excellent reputations—go out of business. How can you protect yourself? First, always pay with a credit card; if you have a problem, your credit-card company may help you resolve it. Second, buy trip insurance that covers default. Third, choose a company that belongs to the United States Tour Operators Association, whose members must set aside funds ($1 million) to cover defaults. Finally choose a company that also participates in the Tour Operator Program of the American Society of Travel Agents (ASTA), which will act as mediator in any disputes. You can also check on the tour operator's reputation among travelers by posting an inquiry on one of the Fodors.com forums.

Travel Agencies

If you use an agent—brick-and-mortar or virtual—you'll pay a fee for the service. And know that the service you get from some online agents isn't comprehensive. For example Expedia or Travelocity don't search for prices on budget airlines like

JetBlue, Southwest, or small foreign carriers. That said, some agents (online or not) *do* have access to fares that are difficult to find otherwise, and the savings can more than make up for any surcharge.

A knowledgeable brick-and-mortar travel agent can be a godsend if you're booking a cruise, a package trip that's not available to you directly, an air pass, or a complicated itinerary including several overseas flights. What's more, travel agents that specialize in a destination may have exclusive access to certain deals and insider information on things such as charter flights. Agents who specialize in types of travelers (senior citizens, gays and lesbians, naturists) or types of trips (cruises, luxury travel, safaris) can also be invaluable.

A top-notch agent planning your trip to Russia will make sure you get the correct visa application and complete it on time; the one booking your cruise may get you a cabin upgrade or arrange to have a bottle of champagne chilling in your cabin when you embark. And complain about the surcharges all you like, but when things don't work out the way you'd hoped, it's nice to have an agent to put things right.

➤**AGENT RESOURCES: American Society of Travel Agents** (ASTA) (tel. 703/739–2782 or 800/965–2782 24-hr hotline, www.astanet.com). **United States Tour Operators Association** (USTOA) (tel. 212/599–6599, www.ustoa.com).

➤**ONLINE AGENTS: Expedia** (www.expedia.com). **Onetravel.com** (www.onetravel.com). **Orbitz** (www.orbitz.com). **Priceline.com** (www.priceline.com). **Travelocity** (www.travelocity.com).

Time

Aruba is in the Atlantic standard time zone, which is one hour later than eastern standard time or four hours earlier than Greenwich mean time. During daylight saving time, between

April and October, Atlantic standard is the same time as eastern daylight time.

Visitor Information

Before leaving home, contact the Aruba Tourism Authority at one of its many offices. On Aruba, the tourist office has free brochures and information officers who are ready to answer any questions you may have, weekdays 7:30 AM–4:30 PM.

The Caribbean Tourism Organization, which has information on the island, is another good resource.

➤**ARUBA INFORMATION: Aruba Tourism Authority** (tel. 800/862–7822, www.aruba.com; L. G. Smith Blvd. 172, Eagle Beach, Aruba, tel. 297/582–3777; 1 Financial Plaza, Suite 136, Fort Lauderdale, FL 33394, tel. 954/767–6477; 3455 Peach Tree Rd. NE, Suite 500, Atlanta, GA 30326, tel. 404/892–7822; 5901 N. Cicero, Suite 301, Chicago, IL, 60646, tel. 773/202–5054; 1000 Harbor Blvd., Ground Level, Weehawken, NJ 07087, tel. 201/330–0800; 12707 North Fwy., Suite 138, Houston, TX 77060-1234, tel. 281/872–7822; Business Centre 5875, Suite 201, Hwy. 7, Vaughan, Ontario, L4L 8Z7, tel. 905/264–3434).

➤**CARIBBEAN-WIDE INFORMATION: Caribbean Tourism Organization** (80 Broad St., New York, NY 10004, tel. 212/635–9530, www.onecaribbean.org; Vigilant House, 120 Wilton Rd., London SW1V 1JZ, tel. 020/7233–8382).

➤**GOVERNMENT ADVISORIES: U.S. Department of State** (Bureau of Consular Affairs, Overseas Citizens Services Office, 2201 C St. NW Washington, DC 20520, tel. 888/407–4747 or 202/501–4444 from overseas, www.travel.state.gov).

Web Sites

We're really proud of our Web site; Fodors.com is a great place to begin any journey. Scan Travel Wire for suggested itineraries, travel deals, restaurant and hotel openings, and other up-to-the-minute info. Check out Booking to research prices and book plane tickets, hotel rooms, rental cars, and vacation packages. Head to Talk for on-the-ground pointers from travelers who frequent our message boards. You can also link to loads of other travel-related resources.

After your trip, be sure to rate the places you visited and share your experiences and travel tips with us and other Fodorites in Travel Ratings and Talk on www.fodors.com.

One of the most helpful sites about Aruba may very well be the island's own www.aruba.com. For information on the Caribbean, visit one of the following: www.onecaribbean.org (the Caribbean Tourism Organization's official site, with many island-specific links); www.caribbeantravel.com (the official Caribbean Hotel Association site); www.caribbeannewspapers.com (with links to newspapers published throughout the Caribbean); www.caribinfo.com (with a directory of Web sites based in or related to the Caribbean and links to local phone directories); www.cruising.org (the Cruise Lines International Association's site, with many ship profiles); www.cananews.com (for Caribbean news).

Weddings

In 2002, the Aruba Parliament passed a law enabling people over the age of 18 to marry as long as they submit the appropriate documents 14 days in advance. Couples are required to submit birth certificates with raised seals, through the mail or in person, to Aruba's Office of the Civil Registry. They also need an apostil—a document proving they are free to marry—from their country of residence.

With so many beautiful spots to choose from, weddings on Aruba are guaranteed to be romantic. And be sure to register for the island's "One Cool Honeymoon" program for special discounts from local businesses. Ask your hotel for more information.

ARUBA WEDDINGS FOR YOU is a small company that helps couples make wedding arrangements in advance. Services include securing a location on the island, submitting legal documents, confirming arrangements with suppliers, decorating the venue, and coordinating the ceremony. You can also check out **ARUBA FAIRY TALES,** another company that arranges weddings.

➤**INFORMATION: Aruba Fairy Tales** (Box 4151, Noord, tel. 297/993–0045, fax 297/583–1511, www.arubafairytales.com). **Aruba Weddings for You** (Nune 92, Paradera, tel. 297/583–7638, fax 297/588–6073, www.arubaweddingsforyou.com).

When to Go

Aruba's high season is traditionally winter—from December 15 to April 14—when northern weather is at its worst. During this season you're guaranteed the most entertainment at resorts and the most people with whom to enjoy it. It's also the most fashionable, the most expensive, and the most popular time to visit—and most hotels are heavily booked. You must make reservations at least two or three months in advance for the very best places. Hotel prices drop 20% to 40% after April 15.

index

FODOR'S POCKET ARUBA

EDITOR: Michael Nalepa

Editorial Contributor: Vernon O'Reilly-Ramesar

Editorial Production: Evangelos Vasilakis

Maps: David Lindroth, *cartographer;* Rebecca Baer and Bob Blake, *map editors*

Design: Fabrizio La Rocca, *creative director;* Tigist Getachew, *art director;* Melanie Marin, *senior picture editor*

Production/Manufacturing: Angela L. McLean

Cover Photograph: Darrell Jones

COPYRIGHT

Fourth Edition

ISBN-10: 1–4000–1697–5

ISBN-13: 978–1–4000–1697–6

ISSN: 1098–2663

SPECIAL SALES

This book is available at special discounts for bulk purchases for sales promotions or premiums. Special editions, including personalized covers, excerpts of existing books, and corporate imprints, can be created in large quantities for special needs. For more information, write to Special Markets/Premium Sales, 1745 Broadway, MD 6-2, New York, NY 10019, or e-mail specialmarkets@randomhouse.com.

AN IMPORTANT TIP & AN INVITATION

Although all prices, opening times, and other details in this book are based on information supplied to us at press time, changes occur all the time in the travel world, and Fodor's cannot accept responsibility for facts that become outdated or for inadvertent errors or omissions. So **always confirm information when it matters,** especially if you're making a detour to visit a specific place. Your experiences—positive and negative—matter to us. If we have missed or misstated something, **please write to us.** We follow up on all suggestions. Contact the Aruba editor at editors@fodors.com or c/o Fodor's at 1745 Broadway, New York, NY 10019.

PRINTED IN THE UNITED STATES OF AMERICA

10 9 8 7 6 5 4 3 2 1